THE
SHADOW
WORK
WORKBOOK

Self-Care Exercises for Healing Your Trauma
and Exploring Your Hidden Self

JOR-EL CARABALLO, LMHC

ADAMS MEDIA
NEW YORK   LONDON   TORONTO   SYDNEY   NEW DELHI

Adams Media
An Imprint of Simon & Schuster, Inc.
100 Technology Center Drive
Stoughton, Massachusetts 02072

First Adams Media trade paperback edition September 2022

ADAMS MEDIA and colophon are trademarks of Simon & Schuster.

For information about special discounts for bulk purchases, please contact Simon & Schuster Special Sales at 1-866-506-1949 or business@simonandschuster.com.

The Simon & Schuster Speakers Bureau can bring authors to your live event. For more information or to book an event contact the Simon & Schuster Speakers Bureau at 1-866-248-3049 or visit our website at www.simonspeakers.com.

Interior design by Colleen Cunningham
Illustrations by Tess Armstrong

Manufactured in the United States of America

4 2023

Library of Congress Cataloging-in-Publication Data
Names: Caraballo, Jor-El, author.
Title: The shadow work workbook / Jor-El Caraballo, LMHC.
Description: First Adams Media trade paperback edition. | Stoughton, Massachusetts: Adams Media, [2022] | Includes bibliographical references and index. Identifiers: LCCN 2022014631 | ISBN 9781507219799 (pb)
Subjects: LCSH: Self-actualization (Psychology) | Self-acceptance. | Self-confidence. | Subconsciousness.
Classification: LCC BF637.S4 C3556 2022 | DDC 158.1--dc23/eng/20220509
LC record available at https://lccn.loc.gov/2022014631

ISBN 978-1-5072-1979-9

For anyone who is also on a journey
of self-discovery and acceptance...
you deserve it.

Contents

Introduction

Have you found yourself struggling with regular bouts of anger, self-critical thoughts, or troubling relationship patterns? If so, then there is likely something you need to explore within your shadow self.

Your shadow self is the place where all your hurts, fears, and sadness have been repressed. These are the parts of you that don't often see the light of day—things that you may be choosing to avoid because they feel too overwhelming. But avoiding these emotions and allowing them to linger unexamined in your shadow is not healthy. It also stops you from ever truly knowing your whole self and achieving the self-love that comes from that acceptance.

But the good news is you can work to better understand and integrate these repressed parts of yourself through shadow work. Shadow work is a form of mental self-care that will help you heal your past wounds so that you can live a better life. This work is not easy, and at times it can bring up emotions or memories that you might rather have kept hidden, but it is necessary if you want to discover who you really are. The forty workbook entries in *The Shadow Work Workbook* will help you better understand your shadow self.

First, each entry will discuss a different aspect of the shadow and provide thought-provoking questions for you to think on and explore. After you've dug deep into those questions, you'll find a series of related affirmations that will drive home the message of self-acceptance and strengthen and fortify the positive thoughts you want your mind to concentrate on.

Some facets of the shadow that you will explore are:

- Meet Your Inner Child
- Offer Self-Forgiveness
- Explore Your Hidden Anger
- Reflect on Your Dreams
- Process Loss
- Sit with Difficult Emotions

With exercises exploring anger and shame, feeling your feelings, and so much more, *The Shadow Work Workbook* helps you gain a deeper love and understanding of all parts of yourself. Shadow work can be the path you need to move past old wounds and make your way forward to living a happier, more fulfilled life.

PART ONE

Introduction to Shadow Work

Welcome to the world of shadow work! Preparation and pacing are critical, yet unspoken, principles of doing hard emotional work. This book is structured in a way to help you be successful at doing shadow work by resting on these therapeutic principles. This will help prevent the work from feeling too difficult and overwhelming.

In this first part, you will read some recommendations on how to best use this book to ensure that you're gaining the insight that you want, while also taking good care of yourself as you do this work. You can be successful by ensuring that you have appropriate supports in place as you begin delving deep into your shadow side. It's also important to continuously self-reflect and take breaks to utilize those resources when you need to. You will find more thoughts on best practices in the upcoming pages.

You will also learn about the role of grounding and why it's central to shadow work. You will discover some grounding exercises to use in preparation of and after your shadow work sessions. Take some time to familiarize yourself with these practices, as they will be your emotional anchor during this kind of self-exploration.

What Is the Shadow?

The idea of the "shadow self" was popularized by Swiss psychoanalyst and psychiatrist Carl Jung. Jung thought of the shadow as the mirror to Sigmund Freud's "unconscious." (Freud, like Jung, believed that the unconscious mind represents the collection of thoughts and feelings we don't readily accessble because they are too painful.) The shadow represents the repressed parts of your personality. These hidden parts are largely negative but may also include positive aspects that you've learned to hide for various reasons. These hidden parts can range from negative feelings (like fear, sadness, and anger) to unspoken truths, deeply held traumas, or pain.

As a part of your psyche (or more simply, your mind), the shadow exists in deep contrast to the persona, which is like "the face that you put on for the world." The persona is the daily mask you wear and what people often think of as your personality. These are the aspects of yourself that you more readily show to others as you go about daily life. If you were to ask a friend, colleague, or loved one to use a few adjectives to describe you, they would use words that reflect your persona and not your deepest inner thoughts and feelings (such as your shadow).

That is no fault of theirs, however, as Jung believed that it is normal for people to have parts of themselves that are hidden from others. And sometimes, when you are in deep denial or pain, these parts even become hidden to you. While this may be a normal part of our existence, it isn't entirely healthy.

What Exists in the Shadow?

For most people, the shadow represents their deepest hurts, fears, and insecurities. The nexus of your anxieties may exist in your shadow self. The shadow most often represents darker emotions such as anger, rage, and frustration that most people find difficult to express in everyday life.

The shadow, however, isn't all bad! Some positive qualities might also exist in this metaphorical part of your brain. Consider the young boy who displays a great sensitivity at a young age or a young girl who learns that she needs to remain quiet to be seen as tolerable and acceptable. We generally think of sensitivity and assertiveness as positive qualities to aspire to, so why might they exist in someone's shadow? When you receive critical feedback about parts of yourself—especially in your younger years—you learn to internalize and hide them. Shame turns those beautiful qualities dark, banishing them to the depths of your shadow self. As you mature, you may find yourself continuously struggling with presenting only your socially acceptable qualities to the world (persona), while you minimize or hide those parts of you that you've learned were simply not okay. You feel confused about the internal turmoil you experience in your life and connections.

It should be said that shadow work is not solely about the things you experience as a child. Adults can minimize painful experiences as well. While no two people may experience a major life event (such as losing a loved one or job, facing discrimination, living through a pandemic, and so on) or trauma in the same way, we often minimize our thoughts, reactions,

and feelings almost automatically. Sometimes this minimization is out of necessity, as you have neither the time, capacity, nor skills required to create space for these feelings. Other
times, you consciously make that choice to simply avoid
what feels too overwhelming. After all, dealing with the most
vulnerable and tender parts of yourself can feel scary and
unnerving. This can be true despite your recognition that
something internal is begging for your support and attention.

Jung's theory of the shadow is built on the following
ideas: First, we *all* have a shadow self, and second, true psychological wellness requires you to integrate these undesirable parts of yourself into your larger personality. This,
in turn, reduces the discomfort and persistent uneasiness,
anxiety, and inner conflict you feel as you walk through life
trying to contort yourself into roles, relationships, and environments that actually do not work for you.

The shadow often represents the parts of yourself that you
refuse to acknowledge. Largely informed by the feedback of
others, your ego seeks to protect these parts and buries them
deep. The ego works hand in hand with the superego, which
manages how you interact with the world around you. Base
level impulses (id) and parts of yourself minimized by others
become relegated to the shadow and unconscious parts of
your mind. Your more conscious parts (ego, superego, persona) drive the car, while the id and shadow self become invis-
ible backseat drivers. This breeds internal tension and conflict.
You consciously identify with your ego. The shadow self then
becomes the unconscious driver of your behavior and choices,
while your conscious self struggles to make sense of why you

do the things that you do. Herein lies the greatest case to be made for doing the personal work to go deeper.

One of the greatest metaphors for the shadow in literature is Robert Louis Stevenson's *Strange Case of Dr. Jekyll and Mr. Hyde*. This dramatized version of the persona (Dr. Jekyll) and the shadow (Mr. Hyde) mimics Jung's theory that within us we all have a range of depth and darkness that we do not readily recognize and accept. Through introspection and integration, Jung believed that we can experience greater quality of life and internal peace alongside our shadow selves. This process allows us to develop greater insight and avoid becoming our own worst critics and saboteurs.

Why You Should Do Shadow Work

Insight and self-awareness are two of the most important tools for mental health and well-being. Shadow work is one of many ways to increase your understanding of yourself, and is an incredibly effective way to deepen your understanding of your hopes and fears.

When you operate with a lack of insight, you can experience unsettling emotions such as confusion, guilt, and shame. Developing more clarity on your deepest wishes and traumas not only enables you to better understand what you want out of life, but also helps you heal. When you heal, you experience greater mental health because you are able to release some of the deep shame and guilt you may have developed in response to difficult circumstances such as trauma, neglect, or abuse. You experience freedom from harmful patterns in your life, such as devoting time to unfulfilling work or toxic relationships. When you better understand what's in your shadow self you can make more informed choices about how to intentionally address your needs and your pain. Without this deep insight, you may continue to experience the same challenges over and over again, oblivious to how (and why) you find yourself stuck in those patterns.

Shadow work is hard, challenging work but it is worth undertaking. On the other side of this work is a fuller integration of all parts of yourself, allowing you to have a greater quality of life with more peace and ease.

Be Prepared for Digging Deep

Gaining a deeper and better understanding of yourself is liberating, affirming work. As you begin to do this work, you may find that negative feelings or memories come up. This is common and even expected. After all, when you take steps to make subconscious (or unconscious) material more conscious, some of the things you don't like thinking or feeling rush to the surface. As you make your way through this book, you should gather any support that you may find helpful. Friends, family, a partner, or other loved ones can be incredible allies on this journey to deep self-discovery and healing. Furthermore, you may find that you want or need more assistance as you make your way through this journey. You might consider eliciting the support of a licensed therapist should you have the means and resources to do so. Of course, not everyone has access to the same resources, so at the back of this book you'll find some networks, websites, books, and more that you may consider using as you learn more about yourself and what you find in your shadow.

While this work can be difficult, it is incredibly transformative and healing. When you find yourself stuck in negative patterns or feeling worn out with your old ways of being, shadow work illuminates a healthier path forward. At times you may feel awkward or uncomfortable. You might even find yourself sad or grieving while doing this work—all of which is relatively common. Try your best to be patient and kind with yourself. Also try to embrace routines and self-care rituals that help you feel grounded.

Beginning Your Shadow Work

Learning more about yourself is a loving gesture. Whether there is a specific situation in your life that's causing you to feel out of sorts, or you're looking for more insight, this book will help you on your journey. The goal of this book is to not only give you information about what the shadow is but also provide some guidance and direction that will help you get closer to leading the life you want to live. This workbook isn't meant to be prescriptive, however, as it can't possibly understand you and your life circumstances better than you do. Rather, this book will help you explore a new world—your inner world—with some new depth and understanding.

The exercises in this book will help you contact, and better understand, your shadow self. The goal is to tap in to the not so readily visible parts of your subconscious. With this new information, you'll be able to tap in to some hidden talents, disrupt subconscious patterns in your life, and reach the next step on your healing path.

The first part of this book provides you with some information on grounding, which is going to be critical in doing this hard work. It is recommended that you pace yourself and do a grounding exercise before completing any entry. This will allow you to center yourself before diving into difficult shadow work. This also helps you shake off any stress that you may be coming to the work with, which can cloud your efforts or possibly leave you feeling unnerved. After you do some grounding, then choose an entry that you'd like to address and work on. You can do the entries in order or select one that feels particularly relevant for your life right now. Read the information provided in each entry, then respond to the questions for reflection, and wrap up your session with the affirmations and potentially more grounding. You may decide to complete more than one entry in one sitting and that's okay too. Just be conscious of checking in with yourself after each entry so as to not overwork yourself. And if you are already feeling worn out, exhausted, frustrated, or upset, that is not the time to do shadow work. You will need energy and courage to dive into shadow work. Set yourself up for success when something else isn't metaphorically standing in your way.

Before you begin, keep the following things in mind.

Take Your Time

Exploring the shadow is hard psychological work, mainly due to our tendency to reject the not-so-wonderful parts of us. It can be tiring to fight your way through the mental roadblocks of internalized messages and anxious or depressive thoughts and feelings. This work takes a lot of energy. This is especially true if you work with the aim of being as honest as possible with yourself. Be sure to take your time and take breaks regularly between exercises. Don't worry, they will be here waiting for you when you return.

Try to Be Patient

When you begin this kind of work, you don't always get crystal clear revelations immediately. Shadow work is often more complicated than that. There may be some topics or exercises in which you'll gain deeper insight much more easily, and others that may feel a bit more challenging. It's okay to acknowledge the progress that you make, but also know that those more challenging topics will likely take more time and patience. Try not to rush or pressure yourself to the point of mental frustration and exhaustion. Shadow work is an ongoing process as you grow. Your thoughts and feelings about yourself, your personal history, and the world around you can change over time. Give yourself time to learn more about you. The insight will come!

Have a Solid Support System

As deep personal work can be taxing, it is critical to ensure that you have ways to support your wellness throughout your use of this workbook. Make sure that you have tried-and-true self-care practices that are accessible. Remember, self-care only works if it's the kind of self-care that you can do.

You may also want to make sure you have other things that bring you joy. Don't get so mired down in "the work" that you forget that you are a person who also needs things that are light and easy. Additionally, please don't underestimate the role of others in your exploration. Other people can be helpful sounding boards for ideas. Friends and loved ones can offer validation of your challenges, as well as a shoulder to cry on if you need it. Professional supports are helpful too. As a mental health professional, I know how transformative and healing therapy can be. Other providers like healers, acupuncturists, Reiki masters, and so on can all provide great support and more insight should you want it. Have supports set up that truly work for you.

Lean Into Self-Compassion

Many people struggle with being kind to themselves, but we all need to learn to embrace self-compassion to be emotionally healthy. Sometimes this can come from deeper understanding of the self, as when you undertake shadow work, but sometimes other practices of self-compassion are needed. This can look like reframing your thoughts, using affirmations, and many other things...like using the entries in this book. Self-acceptance and self-compassion are cornerstones of all the work I do as a mental health professional. My hope is that as you learn to walk alongside your shadow side, self-compassion can become the lens through which you learn to see yourself on that path.

Why Grounding Is Important to Shadow Work

Shadow work involves exploring thoughts and feelings that rest outside of consciousness. It can be difficult, tedious work to move past the daily barriers you set for yourself to avoid the shadow. These barriers, such as denial, repression, and projection, are common strategies to protect yourself from these darker parts of you. They are defensive strategies. You need them in moderate amounts, yet they require extra mental energy to work through.

In addition to the difficulty of sifting through all your psychological defenses, when you get to the core of hidden parts (your shadow) you may not like what you find. After all, those defenses exist so that you do not find yourself completely overwhelmed by your shadow self. When you begin to uncover hidden parts of yourself, you can become shaken and unsettled. As a result, you need strategies and psychological spaces that provide you with security and ease. You need spaces that provide you with respite and moments to recover as you slowly learn to visit with, and integrate, your shadow parts. This is where grounding skills and strategies come in.

The following exercises will provide you with a few options to try out grounding. These will be especially useful if you do not already have tools to help you feel safe and secure with yourself. If you have some previous experience with grounding, some of these strategies may be familiar to you. You may have come across similar versions in your personal development so far. Either way, it is critical that you have these tools on hand as you do this work.

You may experience frustration, hurt, rage, or even despair as you make your way through the pages of this book. It is expected for some difficult feelings to come up as you dive deep into this work. Shadow work is never easy and often unsettling, but is generally manageable if you have access to supports and strategies that help you cope with difficult feelings. Use the grounding exercises that follow as often as you like. Try using them before and after any entry, especially if you find the topic/theme of the exercise to be challenging or triggering.

In addition, if you would like professional support, there are some resources at the end of this book that can be a helpful starting point in working with a licensed therapist.

CONNECT WITH YOUR BREATH

Breathing is a helpful grounding technique that you can use anytime and anywhere. Breath work is incredibly effective at helping you regulate your nervous system, which often becomes activated when you experience challenging feelings like sadness, guilt, shame, and so on. When you do shadow work, you are consciously inviting the possibility for these difficult emotions to come up; therefore, you need tools to help manage stress and overwhelming feelings in the moment. Mindful breathing helps regulate your nervous system, sending the message from your body back to your brain (and your central nervous system) that you are in a safe, secure space free of threats. The following exercise will provide you with a brief introduction to becoming connected with your breath.

Steps to Take

1. **First, take an inventory of the environment around you.** Is this a comfortable and serene space? If not, try to find a space that is more conducive to spending some quiet time with yourself. If you can't be alone, try to use headphones or earplugs, or other ways to limit outside stimulation and distractions from disturbing you.

2. **Next, put yourself in a comfortable position.** You can be seated or lying down in whatever position feels the most comfortable. Just ensure that you can breathe freely and without extra labor or difficulty. You want your diaphragm (belly) and air pathways to be as undisrupted as possible. Make sure that your back is straight, yet also relaxed, whether you are sitting upright or lying down.

3. **Now, take a moment to simply notice what your breath is doing, right here and right now.** Take note of what happens when you inhale and what happens as you exhale. You may notice parts of your body rising on an inhale (like chest, shoulders, stomach) and then deflating as you exhale. Right now, you are just taking notice of what happens with your breath. There is no need to force change.

4. **Breathe in through your nose or through your mouth, whichever feels more comfortable.** Take notice of a few rounds of breaths. You're creating space for yourself, and your breath, just to show up as you are right here, right now. Breathe at whatever rhythm feels comfortable and natural for one minute.

5. **After a minute of natural breathing, try to deepen your breath.** You might find it helpful to gently place a hand on your belly as you do this. As you inhale, allow your belly to expand as your hand rests on it. You will notice that your hand moves outward on this inhale. Allow yourself to breathe noisily too. These breaths might sound like the waves of an ocean; you want these breaths to be nearly as deep.

6. **Try to make each inhale last a few seconds longer, allowing the belly to expand.** Also try to extend your next exhale. Allow your breath to fall out. You will notice that the hand resting on your belly will then contract, coming closer to you on each exhale. Take a minute or so to get used to this deepening breath, noticing how your diaphragm moves through each cycle. You're creating space in the belly for the air to fill, and then releasing it with ease. You do not have to try hard here. Allow the breath to guide you. As you practice more and more, your inhales and exhales will deepen. With practice you will find a breath that feels deeper than your everyday breath but not so much that it feels like labor to do it.

7. **Take a few moments to be with yourself, your body, and this deepening breath.** No judgment. No pressure. Just be connected to the breath that exists in this moment.

8. **When you're ready to re-emerge in your daily life, allow the breath to fall back into its more typical rhythm.** Orient yourself back to the sights and sounds of the space you're in and slowly restart your day.

Know that you've taken just a few minutes to be with yourself and with your breath. Notice how centered and grounded your body feels. Notice how calmness or ease is now your experience. Now you have access to these feelings just with this simple breathing exercise. Use it whenever you like, or when you feel you need to feel a bit more balanced and centered.

CREATE A GROUNDING TOKEN

When you are doing shadow work and facing difficult emotions, you may start to feel stressed or overwhelmed. Therefore, it's important to have different techniques to help you achieve a sense of balance and grounding. Grounding is the process by which you center yourself in the moment to cope with overwhelming anxiety, stress, and even traumatic reactions and dissociation.

One of the most powerful ways that you can ground yourself is to make use of the mind-body connection. You can practice physical grounding by having a small physical token be a part of that process. For this exercise, you will need a small object that can easily fit in your hands. (Typically, the object would be a small stone, a piece of jewelry, a coin, or something of similar size.)

This exercise will help you create a grounding tool, a practical symbol, that you can use in a variety of circumstances, whether you're feeling challenged by shadow work or dealing with some other life stressors.

Steps to Take

1. **First, it's important to create an environment and space that feels comfortable for you.** It's helpful to be in a place with minimal distractions so that you can deeply connect to this grounding experience. Mute or disable notifications on any device that might disrupt you in the next few minutes.

2. **Once you've selected your token and placed yourself in a space that is free of distractions, sit in a comfortable position.** Place your token within arm's reach. You don't need to hold it at this point, but you may wish to. As you settle in, take a minute or two to connect with your breath. If any other thoughts come up as you do this, that's okay. Some busy thoughts can come up. That's normal. Just gently remind yourself for this moment that all you need to do is concentrate on your breath. Spend the next minute or two connecting with your body and your breath.

3. **Once you feel present with your breath and notice that it falls into a gentle, deep rhythm, it's time to imagine a place that you feel best represents tranquility and restfulness.** This may be a place that you've been to before (such as a beautiful beach or the home of a loved one) or it could be a place that exists only in your mind or somewhere in fiction. Fantasy is okay here. The only rule is that this place makes you feel safe and at rest.

4. **Take a moment to imagine the details of this safe environment.** This space might be a beach with warm sand and a gentle breeze. It also might be a space in your home, or a place you've read about or seen in a movie. Capture

the details in your mind, from what the lighting is like to what objects fill the space. Imagine the noises that you might hear in the space, and the other beings (like people or animals) who also might be there to greet you with warmth and kindness. Allow yourself to revel in these details for a moment.

5. **As you gain a clearer picture of this inviting environment, reach for your small token and place it in your hands, allowing it to rest just between your palms.** Your grip should be comfortable, yet firm. Take note of the details of this token resting between your palms. Notice its shape, weight, and texture as it sits within your hands. As you do that, don't lose sight of that restful place in your mind's eye.

6. **Now focus on all that positive healing and relaxed energy as you begin to squeeze the token in your hands for the next thirty seconds.** You are channeling the energy of that warm, restful place into the token you hold between your hands. As you squeeze the token you should feel the tension within your hands, forearms, and upper arms. Imagine that you are pushing the healing energy from this inviting place directly into this token, where the memory of that place will continue to live.

7. **After those thirty seconds, allow your hands to fall back at rest.** Let the token rest in your hands, but without tension.

You have just taken a moment to create a very special token and turned it into a symbol. This small token now represents this moment, this small journey that you've just taken through your mind to that inviting place.

This physical manifestation of that place represents comfort, safety, protection, and ease. You can take this token with you and use it whenever you feel like you need extra support and grounding. You may choose to have this token with you as you complete a shadow work entry. You can even use this token throughout your daily life whenever you're struggling.

This token not only represents the safe place in your mind, but also represents the time that you've taken today to be with yourself, offering the space to feel cared for and looked after. You've just given that gift to yourself!

Feel free to circle back to this exercise with any new token that you'd like to be a grounding tool for you.

USE THE VAULT

The Vault is a grounding exercise that is helpful when you encounter something difficult to deal with in the moment. Shadow work is often about approaching difficult emotions and thoughts. Having the mental space and time to address these concerns, while necessary for this work, is often easier said than done. You may not always have the capacity to address these concerns in the moment. The Vault exercise provides a helpful strategy to manage these kinds of moments.

The Vault is an exercise in envisioning the process of compartmentalizing, or shutting away, difficult emotional material. It's an active choice to "put away" this material until you are better equipped to effectively deal with the challenge it represents. As shadow material often relies on repression to hide from the conscious parts of yourself, the risk with using the Vault is that the repression feels all too comfortable and familiar. The difference here is the Vault is both conscious and temporary. This means that if the Vault is your grounding tool of choice, you should also be intentional to make space to revisit what you temporarily store here. Otherwise, it will remain in a part of your shadow self that you're actively trying to integrate and uncover. Be cautious of the allure of tucking something away in the Vault indefinitely. You can mitigate this by revisiting the specific thought later.

When you're feeling overwhelmed or stressed, you may need to compartmentalize something to stay functional in your daily life. With shadow work, this might mean realizing you've uncovered some traumatic material from your past that you find overwhelming but need to tuck away for the meantime (or until your next therapy appointment). Shadow work often means encountering shadow material in your day-to-day life and having to immediately return to work or show up in some other way. It is unrealistic to suggest that you stop everything to tend to this work. What you can do, however, is have tools to help you get back to a grounding space and regulate your emotions.

Steps to Take

1. **First, make sure that you are in a space that is comfortable enough for you to focus for the next several minutes.** This exercise requires envisioning, so being able to activate

your imagination is essential. This is often impossible with a lot of distractions.

2. **Now, take a moment to identify the distressing thought, feeling, or image that's just come up for you.** This might also be something a bit more amorphous, like an interaction with a person, for example. Imagine this distressing thought or feeling as a physical object, something that you could hold in your hands right in front of you. You might imagine this as a shape at first, like a circle or square—perhaps it is a box that contains the thoughts and feelings you're having trouble with.

3. **Now envision that this object has its own color and texture as well.** This should reflect the difficulty that this object is meant to symbolize. For example, you might envision anger as a bright red box covered in bumps or spikes that make it uncomfortable to hold. Also consider the weight of the object as if you were physically carrying it yourself. Take a moment to settle into your imagination, creating a vivid description of this bothersome object.

4. **Next, visualize that you are carrying this object into a bank.** This bank is old and solid, reminiscent of the time long ago in which it was created. It has tall columns and marble floors that have withstood the test of time. It is formidable.

5. **You make your way past the other patrons and tellers of the bank and walk to a high-security area.** You are recognized by the security staff and are allowed to descend to the basement level. As you reach the bottom you enter a hallway and in the distance you see the bank's large vault.

The vault is roped off and has a large wheel door lock like the ones you've seen in movies. It's made of steel and the door is much taller than you are. The object you carry seems almost minuscule in comparison.

6. **You approach slowly, slightly burdened by the object that you're carrying.** You use the strength of your arms to turn the large wheel lock. You may even have to temporarily place your object on the ground next to you in order to do so. The weight of the door is almost too much for one person, but you somehow manage. The door opens to reveal an expansive room with rows of racks and shelves. Each shelf has a collection of boxes and objects, some like the one you're bringing to deposit. They are all safely stored away.

7. **You approach a shelf and place your object there.** Your body feels immediate relief from being able to lay down your burden. You turn around and exit the vault carefully so as to not disturb the other objects around you. After you exit, you muster up the energy to push the vault door closed, struggling to turn the giant wheel again until you hear a series of clinks and latches falling back into their rightful place. The vault's door is locked and secure again.

8. **You leave the secure area.** You exit the bank and head back into your normal, everyday life.

This object, the symbol of your difficulty, is now safe and secure within the vault. When you think that you have the capacity and resources to effectively tend to it, imagine yourself walking back into the bank, down to the vault, opening the door and so forth.

CREATE YOUR SACRED SPACE

We all need to feel safe. Yet, when you take up the work to explore your shadow self, you intentionally walk into the darkness in the hopes that you will come back feeling more at peace. Taking the journey into the dark corners of your mind is not easy. Feelings like grief, sadness, guilt, and shame come up as you look at yourself with fresh, curious eyes. This can leave you feeling untethered and a bit unsafe.

This is your invitation to imagine an environment or space that feels safe and secure for you. This will be a place of refuge that you can come back to whenever you need respite from this difficult work. Answer these questions in the following space or on a separate piece of paper to help create the vision of your sacred space.

- **What does your space look like from a physical and structural perspective?** Is it a simple room housed within a larger structure? What about a tropical location outdoors? This space could also be a location that doesn't exist in your everyday life. It could be a sacred space that you imagine or may have seen in a movie or TV show that resonated with you. What environment feels safe, secure, and comfortable for you?

- **What comes with this space?** Are there objects that feel familiar or is it all new? Perhaps this sacred space is a room with an altar or personal belongings of significance. Maybe there are walls lined with plants or comfortable furniture upon which you can rest. What do you see displayed within the physical space?

- **What are some thoughts or feelings that come up as you imagine yourself in this space?** And do you notice any changes in your body as you imagine it right now?
- **Within this space, is there anyone else with you that helps you feel safe?** This could be a person (or multiple people) or even pets or other animals.

Now that you've created this sacred space, allow yourself to revisit it whenever you feel like you need some extra grounding. You might even want to visually capture this place with a drawing or collage that helps you reconnect to the feelings of safety this place provides to you.

REFLECT ON PERSONAL HEROES

Shadow work is introspective and, by extension, isolating. Even if some people are there to support you on your journey of self-discovery, they can't completely understand your feelings and thoughts. This is not to suggest that you shouldn't seek out support while doing this work; it's quite the opposite. We all need social, and sometimes professional, support to walk through integrating our shadow selves. However, most of the time you spend doing this work is solitary.

Continued inspiration can help bridge the gap between support you get in real life from those around you, and what your needs are as you undertake shadow work. This is the time to imagine the people who will be your support team. Think of these personal heroes as people you might mentally call upon when you need a little extra support or inspiration.

Your personal heroes can be people from your own life that you find strong and resilient. Maybe there are certain people you know that embody what it means to be a pillar of strength. A personal hero might be a professional, clergy member, or adviser you lean on for support. A personal hero can also be a performer, athlete, or fictional character that embodies perseverance and strength. They can be real people, animated, and even superheroes.

Take a few moments now to reflect on who you can call upon when you need extra support in your journey of self-development, and write their names in the space that follows. With each hero you list, write down a few adjectives that describe how you see this person as an asset to your support team.

PART TWO

Shadow Work Entries

The previous part shared some practical strategies to help ground you as you begin to do shadow work. These kinds of strategies can be helpful before and/or after completing one of the upcoming exercises, or you can use them at any point in your day when you need to feel a bit more in control and grounded.

In this part, you will come across entries to help you get in touch with your shadow self, practice self-care, and identify some steps for your ongoing healing. Each entry begins with some exploration of a shadow work topic or theme. You will see themes related to relationships, exploring safety, and getting in touch with your inner child, among others. Each entry will include a few questions for reflection. This is designed to get you thinking more deeply about your own shadow material. After that, you will see some affirmations to help ground you with self-compassion.

As previously mentioned, shadow work can be difficult, so there's no need to plow through this workbook quickly—go at your own pace. You may want to make your way through every entry in order or you might decide to take a less linear approach and jump around to sections that address more relevant themes in your life first. That's perfectly okay! There is no right or wrong way to do this work. You are making time to take care of your-self and gain more insight and self-awareness, which is the most important thing. Take your time and create space for meaningful reflection with these entries. And, if you need, revisit any of the grounding strategies as often as you like.

GET IN TOUCH WITH YOUR INNER DIALOGUE

We all have an inner voice. To some this may come in the form of thoughts that are easily discernible, while to others that dialogue might come as a feeling or somatic experience. Some people might experience their inner dialogue as their intuition or "gut feelings," while others find it hard to connect with any of these examples.

We are all unique and experience our internal dialogues in different ways. Being connected to this part of yourself is critical as it often provides a wealth of information about your deeper thoughts, feelings, and motivations, all of which drive your perspective on your experiences and how you choose to respond to them.

You may go about your daily life without much conscious thought about your internal dialogue. While the quality of this internal dialogue fuels you (much like fuel for a car), you aren't often aware of what that quality is without taking time to pause and reflect.

How often have you stopped yourself in the middle of some activity and asked, "What's coming up for me right now in this moment? How does this actually feel for me?" Chances are that doesn't happen often. This is true even for those of us who try very hard to stay present. While in some ways that kind of presence is a beautiful way of engaging with the world, it is impractical to think of that as a continuous goal. You experience too much daily to stay present with it all. Your nervous system needs some downtime to coalesce, and make sense of, how you're engaging with your environment.

Taking time to foster a deeper connection with your inner dialogue can yield some impressive results. Learning to tune in more often can provide you with deeper insight into how you're experiencing the world around you and what deeper parts of you might be begging for some attention. When you take the time to pause in this way, you create space for shadow material to reveal itself—allowing you to make more consciously informed decisions about how you can take care of yourself. This insight also tells you what your internal world needs to feel whole and respected.

This exercise is aimed at helping you start or maintain that connection, if that's proven difficult with the daily responsibilities of life. Take a moment to listen to what your inner voice might be telling you. Pay attention to any themes, stories, or scripts that might come up often. Those themes that come up often point to shadow material begging for attention and resolution. And, if you find this section particularly challenging, it might also be helpful to revisit one of the grounding exercises in the first part of this book for more support.

When you think of your inner dialogue, what themes come up often? Is there a general vibe or energy that comes with these internal conversations? How do your thoughts often make you feel?

Does your internal dialogue remind you of anyone you've encountered in the past or still encounter (like a romantic partner, parent, caregiver, or other authority figure)?

Is there anything that you'd like to change about your inner dialogue? What resources can you call upon to help you make that change?

AFFIRMATIONS

I can learn to observe my inner dialogue for greater clarity on my thoughts and feelings.

Having a negative inner dialogue does not mean that I am a negative or bad person.

I can, and will, work to shift my inner voice toward a more compassionate perspective.

I deserve to feel at home and at peace with my thoughts.

EXAMINE YOUR PERSONAL STORIES

Self-deception is truly a human experience. We all have stories we like to tell ourselves. As we live so much of our world inside our own minds, we construct realities based on how we make sense of our world around us. These are our personal stories.

Sometimes these stories can be dramatic and grandiose. Sometimes they can reflect your tendencies to shrink and invalidate your own experiences. You may see yourself as the central character in a complicated story, or the often-ignored sidekick who never gets their due. You intuitively create stories to make sense of your experiences and interactions with others.

You are the center of your own universe. You can't help but see the world through the filter of your own history and experiences. However, if you take the time to recognize the reality that you construct these stories yourself, and that some stories are true and others less so, you can gain deep insight into the ways you deeply feel about yourself.

It is not uncommon for us to hold less-than-accurate views of ourselves. This can work in both positive and negative directions. This is largely because humans are prone to biased ways of thinking. This idea is universal. If you have an inflated sense of self, you may repeatedly tell yourself stories about how smart, good, or attractive you are. If you struggle with negative self-assessment, you might tell yourself stories about how unworthy or weird you are. You may also act out these roles, often externalizing what is deeply hidden within your shadow self.

You form your stories not only by listening to your own self-perception, but also by internalizing the reactions and feedback you get from others. When this shadow material goes unchecked, you can live your life motivated by stories that misrepresent you. You miss out on living who you want to be. For example, if you're repeatedly told that you're not good at math, you're much more likely to tell that story to yourself and others when posed with a math challenge. Some people might be inspired to rise to the challenge, particularly if the potential gains are high. However, if the benefits are only mildly beneficial, most people will simply not try. After all, you're no good at math! But what might happen if you heard a different story? What if you were told you could be good at math? How might that story start to change your self-perception of your own capacity? How might new career opportunities open for you with this new narrative?

Naturally, you may be thinking about how early these stories begin in your life, and how fundamental they can be at shaping your lived reality. We've all been told stories about our gender, sex, or culture. We've been told stories about our roles as siblings and what it means to be a partner. We all carry a range of stories within us. To better understand your shadow side, you need to unearth these stories and check them. Do these stories you carry fit you? What about for your life moving forward?

Try to think of a simple idea that you've always believed to be true. Maybe it was a message about something already mentioned in this entry (like gender) or maybe it's something else. Now, think of that "truth" as less objective and more like a story or script. Who told you that story? What might have motivated their perspective? Do you think they were also told the same story?

What's one story you hold of yourself (from your self-perception)? What if your story is skewed? How could that possibility change how you see yourself?

Ask a friend or loved one to name a personal trait they think you have and what that means to them. Do you also see yourself that way? How might that trait impact your choices and behaviors in your daily life?

What's one negative or painful story that you have about yourself?

AFFIRMATIONS

Every person tells themselves stories
to better understand their place in the
world. I am working to learn my own.

My stories are informed by how I come
to see myself and through the messages
I've internalized from others.

I give myself permission to leave behind
old stories that no longer serve me.

LISTEN TO YOUR INTUITION

Listening to your intuition can be complicated. While many people have some understanding of what intuition means, it is still an elusive idea—most often to people who desperately seek it. This so-called gut feeling is often touted as the solution to all life's problems, but what happens if you have a hard time figuring out what your deep truth is?

Some people experience listening to their intuition as getting a "gut feeling." Maybe you've described it, or had it described to you, this way before. Maybe you've felt a literal sensation in your stomach when faced with a tough choice. That is intuition for some people. Intuition may also feel like a wave of calm, soothing feeling washing over you that makes you say, "I get it now." While the feeling of being in touch with your intuition differs for everyone, there is one thing that is often true for most: Intuition feels true and light. Intuition exists without judgment or criticism. It's only there to help you answer the tough questions. Intuition brings peacefulness and clarity, even if it reveals to you some challenging truth you are about to face.

The shadow can make cultivating or maintaining a relationship with your intuition difficult. You may have to battle through previous traumatic experiences, attachment issues, self-defeat, or a critical voice. This is even more true if you've spent a lot of time disconnected from this deep sense of knowing. Perhaps it was those previous negative experiences that led you to question your intuition in the first place. But if you've suffered abuse or mistreatment at the hands of someone else, particularly someone you were forced to rely on, then your intuition was not broken. You were in an impossible position. You likely didn't have any option to not trust, or go along with, what that person wanted. That is a problem of abuse, not the result of faulty intuition. The good news is that with practice, and a lot of courage, you can develop your intuition and allow it to be the tool that it was designed to be. You may have to do the inner work of healing to build that trust, but once cultivated your intuition can be a guiding force whenever you feel confused or lost in your life. Take some time to reflect on that right now.

Questions for Reflection

Can you identify a moment in life when you felt connected to your intuition and it guided you? How did that feel for you?

What barriers do you have in cultivating or maintaining connection with your intuition?

What do you think will help you maintain connection with your intuition moving forward? What can you practice to cultivate that relationship further?

AFFIRMATIONS

I can find grounding and safety in my intuition.

I can learn to listen to myself again, no matter what I've been through and experienced.

I will learn to take good care of myself by strengthening my relationship with my intuition.

EXPLORE YOUR HIDDEN ANGER

Have you ever had trouble allowing yourself to feel angry? Many of us have a difficult time connecting to and expressing anger. The energy of anger can feel particularly intense as it comes with a sense of force and power that many of us equate with destruction. Anger can be destructive, but much like fire it is a powerful source of energy when wielded properly. Through shadow work, you'll be able to explore the reasons for your anger, your relationship to it, and work to express it in a healthy way.

Despite anger being a normal and healthy human emotion, many of us have grown up in environments that have told us that anger is unrighteous. We are told to believe that anger is destructive and that it must be avoided at all costs. You may have learned that anger is dangerous or scary. Sometimes you get this message about your own anger directly when someone tells you, "You have no reason to be this upset!" At other times this invalidation comes through more indirect messages as you see others, like parents or family members, minimize their own angry feelings.

It should be said that many cultures view anger, and the expression of anger, differently. Some cultures more readily express anger through passionate speech and action, whereas some frown upon any outward expression of displeasure. The cultures and communities you come from shape your relationship with anger. Additionally, the way in which you express anger is modified by the times in which you live, your family dynamics, and even your gender identity (for instance, men are often given more license to be angry and express anger).

If you find that you are quick to anger, then there might be other exercises in this book that will help you tap in to some deeper truths. But even if you believe you do not have a lot of anger, this exercise will help you gain more insight into your personal history with anger and create moments for more reflection.

It is worth noting that the belief that anger is a dangerous emotion is especially true for people who grew up in difficult, or otherwise abusive, family environments. In those environments, it is common to be subjected to unhealthy expressions of anger such as violence. Anger then becomes inextricably linked to the idea that you, as a non-abusive person, are not allowed to access your anger. This is perfect priming for anger to be relegated to the recesses of your shadow self.

Anger is a reasonable emotion. It is often an umbrella emotion, meaning that it covers up deep pain. This can also bring sadness and shame. But anger is justifiable. Anger is a human reaction to a psychological injury. It represents the energy you need to defend yourself and seek righteous resolution. Therefore anger, like any other emotion, deserves space in your life. Without anger you may have a difficult time protecting yourself and making sure that your needs are met.

What previous life experiences do you have with respect to anger, especially in your younger years?

What messages have you received about the acceptability of your anger? What about the anger of others immediately around you? And the greater culture/society at large?

How do you typically react when you recognize that you're angry? Does this differ from the times that you feel sad or hurt?

AFFIRMATIONS

Anger is a normal human emotion.
My anger deserves space and attention.

When I feel anger, it is a sign that some
personal injustice has occurred.

I have a right to feel anger and to
address problems that anger me.

Feeling anger is not unhealthy. I can
make the choice to handle my anger
in a healthy, non-abusive manner.

CARE FOR YOURSELF

Self-care has become a buzzword lately, but what does it actually look like? Being kind to yourself, first and foremost, requires you to believe that care is something you deserve. Sometimes you simply feel undeserving of that kindness and that gets in the way of investing in yourself in compassionate ways. You may think of self-care practices not as parts of daily life, but as otherwise indulgent practices. This is a big hurdle for anyone trying to work through self-deprecating thoughts and scripts that exist within the shadow self.

It is difficult to access those self-critical thoughts that are deeply buried if you aren't connected to them. Then, as your conscious self tries to engage in surface-level self-care practices, you run up against critical self-beliefs that seem insurmountable. Thus, these trendy self-care practices that seem to help others fall short for you, and you might feel defeated as a result. You start to believe that they can't work for you. You personalize this failure, looping in shadow scripts about how faulty and undeserving you are of care. You start to believe that you can't even help yourself. You may believe you are beyond help. This pressure to care for yourself in a way that society has deemed acceptable leaves you feeling even more broken and confused than before.

If this sounds like you then try to consider this entry as a mental experiment as much as it is exploration. Even if at this moment you don't think you are deserving of self-care, try to suspend your disbelief as you engage here and see how it feels. Trust that doing this work in and of itself is self-care.

This belief that you are unworthy of care is a story that many of us have when it comes to caring for ourselves. Somewhere (or in many places more often) in our lives we learned that self-care is indulgent, selfish, and narcissistic. If you've grown up in emotionally minimizing, abusive, or cold environments it can be especially hard to challenge this belief system. These beliefs, however, are very wrong. At its core, self-care is a biological imperative; it is self-preservation in action. It goes well beyond the things that we've come to think of as stereotypical self-care practices. It is not superficial; self-care is not something you can buy in stores. Self-care is deeply nourishing and an act of incredible love.

As society talks more openly about mental health and being active in caring for yourself, you may have also seen a backlash against self-care. This often comes in the form of labeling self-care advocates as too soft or needy. Are these genuine criticisms of this so-called self-care revolution? Is it possible that the pushback is connected to collective shadow material that our society has about our unworthiness of self-compassion?

That cynical line of thinking completely ignores the reality that we all have deep, psychological needs. Self-care is not just about bubble baths and affirmations. As a best practice, self-care is your effort to address your unmet needs. Self-care helps you provide maintenance to your psyche and soul. Self-care helps keep you afloat as you navigate a complex life with complex responsibilities.

What does self-care normally look like for you? What practices help you feel taken care of?

What do you find most difficult about self-care or self-soothing?

What cues or sensations do you observe in yourself that communicate a need for self-care?

What typically gets in the way of giving yourself self-care?

AFFIRMATIONS

Self-care is necessary.

★

I am deserving of self-care and soothing.

★

Self-care is not only about doing what
feels good but also what is necessary.

★

Self-care is an intentional act.

UNLEARN OLD SCRIPTS

What baggage are you carrying that's beginning to feel too heavy?

The shadow is often described as feeling very heavy. Sometimes that weight is because the things that come up are negative and weighty. These things can slow you down from moving forward in your life if you get stuck holding that weight. In other instances, that weight isn't negative per se, but represents just how big and pervasive shadow content can be. Its tentacles reach far and deep into your psyche. It can also, at times, be surprising to realize how much something impacts you even if that impact isn't as simple as being all good or all bad.

The way that you view the world is layered and complex. This perspective is also informed by shadow material, which we often don't recognize. Your worldview is formed by the lessons you encounter very early on in life. The Golden Rule—"Treat others how you want to be treated"—is a good example of one of those lessons. As you get older, the messages get more sophisticated or complex. They stop being as black-and-white for most of us. Your perspectives tend to get a lot muddier.

The lessons you learn early on in your life tend to be simple. They focus on the right actions or right behaviors that you should embody to be a good, kind citizen in the world. Yet, as you get older those messages can become a bit more tainted as you learn to navigate multiple truths simultaneously. For example, you can choose to treat others how you want to be treated, but what about when they don't treat you with the same consideration? How are you to act then? Does that motivate you to reconsider your initial thoughtfulness and choices?

You carry with you stories that change as you experience more in your life. At best, these stories can grow to be more inclusive and compassionate, but no one is perfect. As such, some of these scripts start to become more and more informed by shadow material as you are busy tending to other, more conscious, pursuits.

Whether it is some simple value such as the Golden Rule or some other personal ethos, by taking time to investigate these internal scripts you can gain more insight into what thought systems need reworking. By exploring more deeply you can learn more about how pain has led you to take a different fork in the road than you may have intended. You can now connect with psychological spaces that need healing and identify some thought traps that need to be unlearned along the way.

Are there any themes or patterns in your life that you think require more exploration and investigation? Name them.

What stories do you have about those ideas in your mind? What's your role in perpetuating those scripts (for example, are you active or passive in their maintenance)? What is the role of others around you?

Are there pieces of truth from these scripts that you want to hold on to? What parts need to be unlearned or reworked for a better future?

AFFIRMATIONS

I deserve lightness and to not always
feel burdened by my thoughts.

Introspection is a tool by which I can learn
more about myself and the scripts I repeat.

In the patterns of my life lie some
ideas I need to revisit and rework.

I am capable of the work necessary
to unlearn and start anew.

CONNECT WITH HIDDEN GIFTS

Many people think that the shadow self is all about the hidden, dark, and scary material of our lives. While the shadow is the holding space for that kind of material, it also holds personal gifts and talents that have since been tarnished in your mind.

You were born with unique talents and gifts. Often these gifts reveal themselves as some natural interest that continues to grow over time (when you're offered support and continual encouragement). Even with "natural" talent you need resources to cultivate these gifts. Sadly, not everyone is fortunate enough to have supportive loved ones who foster the development of these traits, talents, or personal gifts.

At times, the minimization of these gifts can be harsh, even manipulative. You can be shamed for being interested in, or gifted in, areas that parents or caregivers don't deem worthwhile. This is a common dynamic when a child wants to seek out creative and performance-based careers only to face discouraging remarks from parents. Most frequently, this invalidation isn't malicious. It's born out of a desire to optimize a child's life and set them up for success in the world. However, what parents who do this fail to realize is that they may be projecting onto their children their own shadow-based narratives about these kinds of pursuits. These concerns often bring up issues related to emotional investment, concerns about financial security, and, unfortunately, sometimes even resentment and envy. The parents' own inner child wounds, often unaddressed, get projected onto their gifted offspring.

With such negative feedback and minimization, the gift, talent, or interest you once held becomes deeply entrenched in your shadow self. These once beautiful parts of you become nothing but distant memories of a younger version of you that you may struggle to establish, and maintain, deep connection with as an adult.

However, you can undertake the work to connect with these gifts hidden in your shadow self. But this doesn't mean that integration requires you to return to things just as they once were. You can reconnect with these gifts and then make a conscious decision if you want to redevelop that connection (in new forms) or decide that you ultimately no longer need these talents in the same way. People grow and change, and so do their interests. You can choose to carry these gifts or talents forward in a way that best suits a healed, adult version of yourself or you can leave them behind. The most important part to recognize is that you have the choice of how you want to move forward with your gifts and talents, without anxiety or fear of retribution. The decision to cultivate these talents is yours alone.

Were there gifts, interests, or goals (or traits) that you had when you were younger that you've lost contact with over the years? What are they?

What do you think has created distance between yourself and these gifts?

In what ways could you reconnect to these things you previously found inspiring and joyful? Might there be a version that could exist now even if it doesn't quite look the same as it was before?

AFFIRMATIONS

Gifts and talents are personal truths
that deserve space in my life.

Reconnecting with interests from
my younger years helps me connect
to a deeper part of myself.

My gifts or talents do not need to be validated
by others to be valuable or worthy.

I can make space for these gifts in
my life now and move forward.

EXPLORE YOUR FAMILY OF ORIGIN

Where you come from—your heritage—greatly informs the person you become as an adult. This likely isn't a revelatory idea for you, especially if you've done some introspective work in trying to better understand yourself, your values, and where your perspectives come from.

Your family of origin refers to the family into which you were born and/or raised. For a lot of people, there is one concrete family of origin. Some of the people in this family may shift over time as relationships change and relatives are brought in, leave, or pass away. However, it's not uncommon for people to experience more than one family of origin, especially if they experienced major life shifts early on, like parental death, adoption, and so on.

Every family unit has its own way of working; some families are stable and highly functional while others are not. Some families include one parent and no siblings, while others include a grandparent as the primary guardian along with siblings or half-siblings. The configurations are unique and dynamic, but the connecting thread is that so much of who you are starts with the environment in which you were raised, for better and for worse.

We often minimize the impact of our family of origin. The worldviews and behaviors that you hold as an adult are informed by your experiences within your family of origin. Sometimes inherited perspectives can be hard to notice, especially for people who move out of their family homes in their adult years. While you are an incredibly unique being on your own, most people underestimate how those early life experiences influence their choices. As such, you may be missing some very important connections to your present-day actions and choices if you don't dig deeper and understand themes and patterns within your family of origin. These influences can be unique to your specific family experiences and be part of your individual consciousness, but can also be represented in the collective unconscious and ancestral lineage.

For example, imagine that you often feel anxious about having enough money. You spend a lot of time thinking about how to make more money, or save it, because you think there is an ongoing threat of financial catastrophe. But how might this anxiety be informed by your family of origin? Perhaps you spent your early years in a low-income household and often overheard your caregivers' concerns about paying the bills. Maybe you even regularly experienced food instability or disconnected utilities as a result. Conversely, maybe you grew up with a parent who made a lot of money for as long as you can remember. Maybe you internalized their anxieties about somehow losing it all and vowed to never find yourself in a destitute position.

Whether these thoughts are about money or some other important life area (marriage, children, accomplishments, etc.), we all have shadow content that we don't acknowledge in our daily lives. We simply go about and do what needs to be done, not understanding the foundation for our daily fears and anxieties. Here is an opportunity to explore more deeply.

When you think of your family of origin (the people with whom you spent most of your formative years), what are the initial feelings and thoughts that come to mind? Are there any sensations you notice in your body as you begin to reflect? Write down a few adjectives that come up.

Consider the financial example discussed in this entry: What thoughts and feelings came up when you thought about your own finances and management of resources? How might your early life experiences be impacting choices and beliefs around money for you today?

Think about an important life area that you've been focusing more on lately (relationships, education, work, and so on). What are some values or beliefs you hold about that topic? Were the same values present in your family? Are yours different? How so?

AFFIRMATIONS

My family provided me with a foundation
for understanding the world.

My family values are ideas, themes, and patterns
that shape how I look at the world as an adult.

I will explore my family's role in my worldview
and empower myself to make conscious
choices of which patterns and themes to carry
forward and which ones to let go of or adjust.

MEET YOUR INNER CHILD

If you've done a bit of exploring when it comes to shadow work, then you've likely come across the idea of inner child work. If you haven't, then this entry will introduce you to what is often considered one of the more foundational theories in connecting to your shadow self.

It is common for people to think of shadow work as getting into contact with your inner child, or the parts of yourself that have missed out on some foundational emotional needs. But, as you will learn throughout this book, shadow work is not simply about contacting the inner child. To suggest that minimizes all the other experiences that we continue to face in our lives that form and change us. Nonetheless, there is room to interact with these younger parts of yourself that so often have unfulfilled needs.

The central concept of the inner child is that you, as an adult, have within your psyche a much younger part of yourself represented as the inner child. It represents the parts of yourself that interacted with the world in your younger years. It's the part of you who depended on parents and primary caregivers for food, shelter, and all your emotional needs and protection. Naturally, as you get older, you lose touch with these parts of yourself. It should be noted that memory plays a role as you tend to forget moments that you experienced as a young child and replace them with other important events that come along as you grow and mature. As a result, your perceptions of self often tend to change.

Sometimes, however, you can experience residual feelings (and thought patterns) that were formed and imprinted upon you in prime developmental years. When certain needs are unmet or unaddressed as adults, there is a lot of space to rationalize and process them more fully. However, as young people with a still-developing brain you don't have the same capacity to conduct deep analysis and formulate meaning of why things happen to you.

Difficult experiences and traumatic events that occur at specific developmental stages can interrupt emotional development processes. As a result, it is not uncommon for inner child work to center around feeling stuck in some way, often related to the themes of safety, trust, and authority figures, to name a few. Of course, this is by no means an exhaustive list of what might come up for you as you try to contact your inner child.

As you reflect on the upcoming questions, take a moment to imagine that there is a younger version of you buried deep within you. That child is not driven so much by high-level rational thought, but more so raw emotion. As you may know, children can be singularly focused and demanding at times. They may also be incredibly sweet and passive. Almost always children are much more vulnerable, and tender, than we are as adults. Take a few breaths and try to tap in to this tenderness as you begin to explore the needs of your inner child.

As you contact your inner child, especially for the first time, what feelings and thoughts initially come up for you? What is your first impression of this younger version of you? Take a moment to describe them.

As you visit with this younger version of you a bit more closely, try to make contact with the role of fun and play in their life. What were their joyous interests? How did they have the most fun?

What lingering feelings or thoughts do you think your inner child carries with you today?

AFFIRMATIONS

My inner child is always with me and
deserves care, love, and affirmation.

When I make time to pause and contact my inner
child self, I can learn more about what joy feels
like. I can also learn what pains linger inside me.

My inner child is a rich source of
shadow material, and their thoughts and
feelings are a part of my adult self.

EXPLORE THE PEOPLE YOU ATTRACT

Relationships take up a lot of space in your life. Whether you spend time working on them, being concerned about them, or trying to avoid them, it's clear that relationships are significant parts of your life. It's not uncommon for them to also be rife with shadow material.

As a therapist, I spend a lot of time talking with people about relationships, and one concern that often comes up is, "Why do I keep attracting the same people?" Maybe this is something you've found yourself wondering at different stages in your life or even right now. It's likely that there's a deep reason you find yourself surrounded by the same kind of person despite your best efforts.

Your subconscious mind is a powerful force. Consciously, you may find yourself trying to avoid a certain type of person to date, but you find this same kind of person in your circle time and time again. You feel stuck and confused and don't know what you've done wrong. It's not at all uncommon to fall into self-criticism and blame. But it's more productive to take a step back and be curious about what might lie just outside your consciousness.

Unbeknownst to you, your brain works in the background, making deeper connections and creating shortcuts that help you work more efficiently. It also coalesces emotional and psychological material to help you make meaning of your experiences (but only if you decide to do the work of decoding the data). When it comes to attracting partners, you may find yourself consistently around the same kind of person because there is something about that type that your brain, maybe even your spirit, finds familiar. This may cause you to feel an internal sense of comfort, even if the relationship looks bad on the surface. You may continue to feel a pull toward this kind of person because you have unfinished business with a similar type of person in your history. This type represents a symbol for shadow material.

If shadow material represents the things about you that you'd like to avoid, or have trouble accepting, then it's likely that you've tried to create distance from past relationship pain. However, just as you might find your personality quirks reflected in the actions of an acquaintance, the people you attract (or more readily pay attention to) can also be incredibly revealing about hidden pain that requires your time and attention. If you find yourself consistently attracted to the same type, consider this your permission to take a deeper look into your shadow and explore why. Be curious; explore and learn what parts of your past your shadow is trying to work through when you aren't quite so conscious of it.

Have you found yourself attracted to the same kind of person repeatedly or stuck in a pattern in your romantic relationships? Take a moment to identify that pattern. Put a name to it.

As you think about this pattern further, what do you think your shadow is trying to draw your attention to?

How do you think you can start to make space to work through this? What's an action step that you can take to work toward interrupting this pattern?

AFFIRMATIONS

I have all the knowledge within me to
understand my relational patterns and themes.

I can move toward learning about myself,
and my choices, without shame.

I have the power within me to work toward
healthier relationships and partners.

FIND BALANCE WITH YOUR SHADOW TRAITS

Chances are that you've come to shadow work because you've felt stuck in your life. You're looking for more insight so you can continue to close the gap between where you are right now and where you'd like to be.

You may have discovered that you struggle with a harsh internal voice or that your inner child desperately needs more love and attention than you've been giving it. I hope that you've been able to learn more about yourself thus far on this journey. I hope that you also understand that not everything about your shadow is something to be corrected or adjusted. Sometimes it's important to acknowledge and accept what your shadow reveals.

Just like the Chinese concepts of yin and yang, most (if not all) things in nature exist in balance. This is also true for whatever resides within you. While you may be working on parts of yourself that need healing in your shadow work, you should also consider how the darker sides of your personality offer their own benefits.

While it may be tempting to think of something that you experience as challenging as completely bad, you should remember that everything that you do in life serves a purpose for you. Otherwise, the thoughts or actions you act on would simply cease to exist. You only continue to rely on choices for which you get reinforcement—even if it's been difficult for you to see their benefits thus far.

Parts of your shadow offer some incredible benefits, even if they pose their own challenges. For example, if you often find yourself struggling to find balance between meeting your own needs and meeting the needs of others, you may experience a great deal of anxiety. On the other hand, this perspective gives you an incredible sense of empathy that helps you show up for the people in your life in ways that perhaps other people cannot or do not.

That is not to say that all your actions should be motivated by self-sacrifice. You do not have to be a martyr to be a good person. But all things must exist in relative balance. You may ebb and flow in your focus on yourself versus a focus on the needs of others, but you should have a sort of emotional home place where you are grounded in having your needs met. At the same time, you don't have to lose access to that part of you that shows up for people in powerful ways. Perhaps it just needs to be checked periodically for balance.

Take a moment to consider how the shadow helps you by looking at the other side of your negative traits.

What's one negative trait or pattern that you've identified within yourself through your shadow work thus far? How does this trait negatively impact, or otherwise disrupt, your life?

Take a moment to reflect on what you gain from this perspective. What might be reinforcing this perspective or action, causing it to persist in your life?

Now, take a moment to offer yourself some compassion. What can you say to yourself to acknowledge the challenge of this part of your shadow self while still embracing its gift?

AFFIRMATIONS

I can make space for the natural ebb and flow of my positive and negative qualities.

Just like all that exists in nature, all that rests within me has the capacity for balance.

I can take the opportunity to gain insight and resolution even from parts of myself that I do not like.

EXPLORE YOUR FEELINGS ABOUT SUCCESS

It can be incredibly exciting to finally be approaching big personal goals. When you find yourself with relative success, a lot of positive thoughts and feelings can come up. Sometimes, however, these moments can also be bittersweet.

It is normal to feel multiple emotions at once. As I often say to my clients, "More than one thing can be true at the same time." When you start to approach a new personal or professional goal, shadow material may also activate. It is not uncommon to experience a wide range of feelings. You may be excited yet nervous, or both happy and in disbelief.

Periods of transition are important times in your life and it's not uncommon to experience ambivalence. How you respond to these moments, and how you respond to change, illuminates deeply held feelings about change, routine, and security. As they relate to charting new territory in your personal life or career, questions of worthiness and deservedness may also come up.

Some people find it easier to simply roll with the punches when changes arrive, and most people tend to do that when things are moving in a positive direction. However, even positive changes come with their complexities. Most notably, if you have struggled with low self-confidence or self-esteem, your shadow self can come to the forefront when positive things happen in your life. Instead of being simply over the moon about the wonderful things coming your way, you instead start to experience a more complex feeling. Anxieties or fears shoot up into your conscious thoughts, seemingly out of nowhere.

You may start to question whether you are deserving of this progress. On the other hand, you might feel very confident in your path toward the goal, but then immediately begin to fear that something terrible might happen to disrupt all that you've worked for. This beautiful new experience quickly becomes tainted. You may cycle through this kind of thought process, this back-and-forth between anxiety and joy, as you perpetually set goals, reach them, set new ones, and so on.

It is normal to have more than one emotion simultaneously. Think of it as your shadow self revealing some pain points that still require your investigation and support. With further reflection you can gain more insight into the "why" behind these bittersweet feelings. Then you will be equipped to better identify the next steps that will help minimize these feelings and prevent them from coming back full force in the future. Take a moment to reflect on the following questions.

How does it feel to be approaching/getting the things that you have wanted for your life? Is there any fear or anxiety related to this success? If so, where might the roots of those feelings be? Have you experienced big gains and losses before?

In what ways do you think this previous experience influences your current choices and perspectives?

How might you try to integrate this shadow material and stay more present with your achievements moving forward?

AFFIRMATIONS

It is common, and valid, to experience
more than one feeling at a time.

Positive steps forward often come
with bittersweet feelings. I can feel
these things and still be grateful.

I can learn more about my relationship
to change and use that information to
create a better future for myself.

REFLECT ON YOUR DREAMS

Dream analysis is common in doing shadow work. Neurologist and psychoanalyst Sigmund Freud popularized the idea that we can find the secrets to our deeper selves through analyzing dreams. Freud believed that dreams were the language of the unconscious. Many in traditional analytical circles believe the same. There are some common themes in our collective understanding of what certain symbols mean according to these philosophies, and you'll learn more about that in a later exercise in this book. Beyond that, many contemporary mental health professionals and spiritual guides believe that by better understanding dreams we can better understand ourselves. But why is that?

During your waking hours, your conscious mind reigns supreme. You largely move according to your conscious thoughts and feelings. You handle the tasks of everyday life. You make intentional choices in navigating your circumstances. You adhere to schedules (or don't) and keep things moving along. For most of us, it's not common to take a step back to understand how the activities of everyday life deeply fulfill us or leave us feeling dissatisfied. We don't often make time to reflect on the purpose and meaning of simple exchanges and interactions because we simply lack the time and capacity to do deeper reflection. To do that kind of introspection, you must make dedicated time to do so (often at the expense of some other tasks or obligations).

As a result, deeper thoughts and feelings get relegated to your shadow or the individual unconscious. Common defense mechanisms like denial, projection, and overcompensation keep you protected from connecting to how and what you are processing (and feeling) about your encounters. These defenses work in the background, saving you mental energy in some instances by focusing on what's most important for the present moment and protecting you from pain you experience in other moments. Unaddressed psychic gunk gets relegated to your shadow, and thus your dreams, via repression.

At this point you might be wondering: Why does all this material come up in your psyche in all these bizarre symbolic ways? It's because when you are unconscious, these defenses don't work as well. When you are asleep, you don't have the same psychological shields of the conscious mind. As the brain tries to process, and make sense of, all the day's events, thoughts, and feelings, they come up in jumbled, symbolic, and distorted ways. We call those experiences dreams!

Dream analysis can be complex, and most professionals have very different thoughts on how dreams work and what the content of dreams means for the collective, as well as for the individual. I believe that there is no singular way to understand dreams. Universal symbols and themes can be a helpful starting point, but an accurate analysis is less about *what* you dream of and more about how you make *meaning* of the dreams for yourself. After all, it is how you make sense of your dreams that motivates you to make different choices in your waking hours.

Take a moment now to think of a recent dream that you can remember and reflect on its meaning.

Questions for Reflection

Before you get into the content of the dream, take a moment to reflect on how it felt for you both within the dream and when you awakened. What feelings or sensations came up? Was there a sense of lightness or darkness? Weightiness or levity?

Now take a moment to reflect on the characters present in a recent dream. Who (or what) showed up in your dreams? What roles do those characters have in your waking life? What might they symbolize?

As you reflect on more of the content of the dream, consider how the central theme or conflict might be reminiscent of something that's happening in your waking life. What comes up for you?

How might you use these reflections to adjust your life during waking hours?

AFFIRMATIONS

Sometimes dreams are very clear
replays of waking life, and at other times,
they can be much more abstract.

By better understanding my dreams, I can
better understand hidden parts of myself.

My dreams have meaning that reflect
my own life and no one else's. They are
for me to understand and learn from.

OFFER SELF-FORGIVENESS

Forgiveness is a virtuous ideal. You may have grown up with people around you extolling forgiveness as a critical part of being a good person. This is helpful, as you may recognize the vast amount of hurt and pain that exists in the world around you. You start to see yourself as a vessel for enriching the lives of others. But how often do you intentionally offer yourself the same kindness and compassion you're so willing to extend to others?

Maybe you weren't taught the benefits of self-compassion and forgiveness. It's possible that the people that helped you grow and mature (like parents, teachers, role models, and so on) didn't have the skills to help you practice forgiveness toward yourself, as it was something that they also struggled with. After all, you can only take someone down a path that you've traveled yourself. As such, you may find that at this point in your life, as you undertake shadow work, that there is a great need to offer yourself the forgiveness you so readily dole out to your partner, family, friends, or even colleagues.

It is hard to offer yourself the kind of forgiveness that you need when you think that the things you've done are despicable or hurt someone else. But every human on this earth makes mistakes. You are no different. You deserve the same kind of compassion and forgiveness that you were taught to extend outward. You deserve that gift just as much as the people around you.

Have you ever found yourself saying, "I'm my own worst critic"? This is cliché for a reason: It's almost normal and expected to be fighting an internal war with a horrible inner critic. If this resonates with you, it's likely that there is something (or many things) that you hold within your shadow that might make offering yourself forgiveness seem disingenuous. It's likely that you have been hard on yourself for such a long time that it now feels abnormal to even think about treating yourself with the kindness that you might readily extend to a stranger. How backward is that?

Begin to see yourself as someone who is capable of doing wrong, but not someone who exists as a wrong or worthless human being. Turn a new page and start to move toward self-forgiveness. This may be a long journey, but every goal begins with taking the first step. Now is the time for you.

How often do you struggle with giving yourself permission to lean into forgiveness and self-compassion?

How does your past, and your previous experiences in relation to others, impact how you see yourself and your capacity for forgiveness?

Take a moment to offer yourself some self-forgiveness right now. Recite: "Right now, I work to forgive myself for _____." How does that feel to say aloud? What challenging thoughts or feelings get in the way of accepting that forgiveness?

AFFIRMATIONS

I am worthy of forgiveness.

Just as I offer compassion to others, I can begin to actively practice self-forgiveness.

I will work to help my internal voice become more neutral and forgiving moving forward.

EXAMINE WHY YOU HOLD A GRUDGE

How often do you find yourself holding a grudge against someone who has wronged you?

Anger is one of those feelings that come up as you think about how someone in your life has disappointed or betrayed you. When you don't get the kind of resolution or apology that you feel you deserve, you can hold on to that anger for an indefinite amount of time. That might lead you to hold a grudge, continuously resenting that person for their misguided behavior. These feelings subconsciously stay in the back of your mind.

As previously mentioned, anger reflects a personal injury that you've been forced to endure at the hands of someone else. When you are fortunate, and integrated, enough to be able to share that anger with the person who wronged you, you get the opportunity to feel a great deal of relief. This sensation is catharsis, which can be healing in and of itself. However, that sort of expression may not leave you feeling whole and respected again, despite your best efforts. When faced with a lack of acknowledgment or no intention to make amends from the other person, you can't come to a peaceful resolution with that feeling. You are left unsettled.

You may have experienced a conflict with someone and used your voice to express your hurt about something they did, but found no resolution. Maybe you were met with defensiveness, excuses, or other complicated rationales that felt like avoiding accountability on the other person's part.

Maybe you walked away from that conversation feeling low and regretting ever having said anything. It's not uncommon for this kind of experience to trigger negative thoughts normally hidden within your shadow. This kind of response can be devastating. You may start to doubt if your assessment of the situation was accurate and if you were entitled to feel that anger in the first place, much less express it. This can easily feed into shadow-informed thought loops of self-doubt, self-criticism, and gaslighting.

This response can also inspire resentment and a grudge that you carry within you for a long time. These negative feelings fester, and you continue to see the offending person as the harbinger of the pain you still carry. They start to become a symbol or an avatar for that pain. Even when you just think of this person, or that previous experience with them, you likely become irritable and negative. You may even have a difficult time seeing them as the person they were to you before the hurt, despite your best attempts to move forward.

These experiences can also be the light shining into a dark corner of your shadow self. These ongoing negative thoughts and feelings often provide the inspiration for fantasies of revenge. It's not uncommon to wish the same sort of emotional (and sometimes physical) pain that you've endured onto the person who is responsible for your hurt. Integrating the shadow means understanding and accepting that it is okay to have those thoughts and feelings. You can fantasize about that revenge without acting on it, and those fantasies do not make you a horrible monster. It just means you are a hurting human being.

How does holding a grudge manifest in your life? How have you noticed that it's changed your behavior in relation to other people (the offending party and others)?

How does this grudge impact your mood or sense of self?

What are your hopes for potential resolution or healing? What do you wish could happen next with this situation?

AFFIRMATIONS

I can make space for the pain
and hurt I carry with me.

Pain has no timeline. Neither does healing.

Having dark thoughts about revenge
does not make me an evil, dark
person. It means I am human.

I can continue to move forward without
pressuring myself to be fully healed.

TURN THE BAD INTO THE GOOD

We often feel compelled to turn all negative feelings and experiences into positive ones. Of course, this can make you feel better, but integrating the shadow means accepting that sometimes experiences can't be made good. Maybe the positives are minimal or perhaps there is no silver lining at all.

Have you ever found yourself in the middle of a difficult moment in your life, wishing that you could get out of the dark hole that you found yourself in? It's a struggle to be in, and live with, those moments. You may think that the hurt and pain you're experiencing will never end. You may feel exhausted by the burdens of your feelings and even depressed and unsure of what steps to take to move forward. This can create the sense of feeling trapped, which undoubtedly can bring up a lot of negative thoughts that are difficult to face.

In situations like this, when you are faced with a challenge that seems insurmountable, it might seem like the solution is to simply shift your perspective. You tell yourself, "No worries. Everything is fine. I'm good!" Sometimes this kind of pep talk is just what you need to continue to push through; however, that may not always be the case.

Denying your feelings is one defense mechanism you can use to handle difficult times in your life. But, just like repression and projection, this kind of skill must be used consciously, whenever possible. If not, you create a pattern of behavior in which you always rely on this one state of being to deny your feelings.

Whether you push your feelings down (repression) or try to act as if they don't exist (denial), they don't exactly go anywhere. These feelings—this hurt that you're feeling and struggling with—still exist inside of you. It might be helpful to get momentary relief to move forward and that's okay; however, if you don't make space and time for healing those feelings at some point, they resurface all on their own. You end up coping with that denied pain in very unhealthy ways. This can lead to troubled relationships and long-standing mental health and substance abuse issues. All of this denied hurt and pain gets stuffed down into the shadow, which is relatively nondisruptive when you validate it and address all the material within it.

What role do you think denial has played in your life? As you were growing up, what messages did you receive about responding to hardship and looking for the silver lining?

What have you been feeling internal pressure to deny, make better, and turn positive?

How can you create space for the weight and hurt without trying to fix it?

AFFIRMATIONS

I can feel hurt and still move forward in my life.

★

I do not need to feel pressure to always
find a silver living in difficult situations.

★

I do not need to feel shame for
struggling or facing difficult times.

DISCOVER HOPE WITH THE MIRACLE QUESTION

When you begin shadow work it's common to feel scared and potentially overwhelmed by what you might face. This hesitancy is what often keeps people from accessing the kind of healing they desperately need. Beginning to investigate yourself can feel daunting and heavy, despite the understanding that this kind of exploration will ultimately place you on a path toward more liberation and healing on the other side.

It can be difficult to feel hopeful that this kind of personal examination will lead you to a mental space that is fruitful and help you weave through the complexities of the rest of your life with ease, but this is precisely what shadow work offers. It offers a pathway for you to see beyond that disorganized hurt and pain that you have been carrying for a long time (maybe without even truly knowing it) and move forward with greater insight, clarity, and focus on what life needs to be for you. While the exercises in this book can be difficult to face and work through, they are designed to give you hope that there is a pathway through the hard times, through the darkness, toward a life that has your lightness and darkness in manageable balance. That is what the miracle question seeks to activate—the idea of hope and a future with new possibilities and balance. Traditionally, the miracle question sounds something like this: "Imagine that you go to sleep tonight, then wake up tomorrow and miraculously you discover a concern of yours is gone. What is now different about your life? How would that feel for you?"

If you've been struggling with negative thoughts and feelings for a long time, this idea of balance and hope may seem too far-fetched, miraculous even. It's okay to approach this kind of personal development with a healthy level of skepticism and disbelief. The goal here is to work with that resistance and keep pushing through, knowing that some of the things you've tried before haven't allowed you to go deep enough to get to the healing that you need. Approach this work with hope for new possibilities, regardless of how unlikely that might seem right now.

Some form of the miracle question has been floating around for some time. As it relates to shadow work, sometimes when you are in the throes of dealing with difficult material, you might forget that on the other side of that depth and darkness is light. You can explore your shadow self, and imagine a future walking alongside these often-hidden parts. This is a crucial part in the path toward integration— being able to imagine a future that exists alongside with, and accepts, the shadow and all that it represents.

On a scale from 1 to 10, with 1 being the least hopeful and 10 being the most hopeful, where do you find yourself right now as you think about the possibilities ahead?

What do you think are your current barriers to hope and envisioning a new future? By contrast, what is present in your life that offers you glimpses of a new path ahead?

Take a moment to imagine that you were able to wake up tomorrow, with deep acceptance and integration of your shadow self. How would your world look different? How would you be changed?

AFFIRMATIONS

Shadow work can be difficult, but I
know that on the other side of this
work is more peace and healing.

I can make space for my hesitancy
and skepticism in doing this work
and still move forward.

I will give myself permission to hope that new
feelings, and new beginnings, lay before me.

EXPLORE LOVE AND HATE

As you may have noticed, exploring the shadow self often means looking for things about yourself that aren't apparent in your everyday life. By examining the differences between the light and the dark, you can more fully grasp and accept what the shadow means to you. Shadow work often means looking at dichotomies, or things that we often think of as opposites, such as light versus darkness and love versus hate.

It is typically much easier for you to think of the things and people that you like and love rather than those you hate. Even as you're reading this now, you may start to reflect on the people in your life that you love or the things that bring you the most joy. You might think of pets or even hobbies that bring up feelings of love for you. This is the light. The dark can be harder to hold and access. You might even find yourself struggling to sit with the possibility of hating someone or something.

Your darkness holds hate and disgust. Most people do not like to think about hating someone or something. You may have been brought up in a family environment that strongly discouraged that word on any and all fronts. It is, of course, healthier to be driven to act out of love rather than hate. Yet, this is a moral evaluation—one born out of the tenets of the collective consciousness of absolutism and purity. This moral evaluation limits your ability to connect with the ugliness of your own personal shadow. It limits your access to the very real feelings of disgust that exist within your shadow self.

Whether or not you grew up in an environment that readily banished hate as a concept, you also get messages every day about how wrong it is to hate. You are likely uncomfortable with how dark it feels to even consider hatred. But acknowledging this part of your shadow self offers you freedom. If you can be present with and accept the negative feelings like hate, disgust, or disdain, something beautiful begins to happen. When you acknowledge this dark side of your own humanity and consciously understand it to be unintegrated shadow material, then you reduce the chance of subconsciously acting out from that hate. You can begin to accept these as shadow thoughts and feelings, not behaviors to be acted out compulsively. With no hatred or vitriol to be repressed, there is no room for the explosive acts of abuse and violence.

If you understand how this hatred can be reflective of some of your deepest inner thoughts, your own pains and traumas, then you can respond to yourself with compassion and healing, rather than projecting your pain outward onto undeserving others.

Do you have trouble allowing yourself to acknowledge hatred or disdain you have for others? Why or why not?

What lessons have you received about these kinds of thoughts and feelings throughout your life?

How does it feel for you, at this moment, to consider acknowledging these feelings?

Is there a specific person, group of people, or idea that you're currently feeling conflicted about? How might this conflict represent projected shadow material of your own?

AFFIRMATIONS

To better integrate my shadow, I will work
toward accepting the light and the dark within.

Hate, disgust, and disdain are feelings
and they do not require action.

I can create space for these negative
feelings to find ways to heal my own pain.

BODY MAP YOUR FEELINGS

Just as dreams are the language of the unconscious, your body has its own stories to tell. In addition to strategies like dream analysis, meditation, journaling, and other spiritual inquiries, you gain more insight into your shadow self by developing a closer relationship with your own physical body.

Your body is the vessel that carries you throughout this world. It automatically absorbs all your experiences. It's with you as you celebrate life's beautiful moments, and it's subjected to life's challenges and traumas. You also receive messages about how your body is supposed to look and function, typically for the benefit and ease of others. With all these complexities, it's easy to get further away from appreciating the body that you have and miss out on valuable information it can provide. The relationship between body and mind is complex.

It can be difficult to be in closer contact with your body if it hasn't been a safe or comfortable place. This is especially true for survivors of abuse, those with disabilities, and people who live with chronic pain and other conditions. If you've spent a lot of time connected to the pain and discomfort of your body, connecting to the body for the sake of self-development can be threatening. If that's the case for you, feel free to revisit this section when you are able.

The mind-body connection tells you that how you feel emotionally is connected to how you feel physically in your body. Your body, and how you experience it, impacts your emotional health. Your emotional health also impacts how you perceive your body. With some training, you can learn to match internal emotional experiences (feelings) to actual physical locations and sensations on the body. For example, if you've ever heard the phrase "I've got a gut feeling," then you already have a basic understanding of this concept. When you feel positively about a situation, this feeling may be warm or relaxing. By contrast, that gut feeling can feel like a sharp jab in the stomach or queasiness when you don't find yourself in a good, safe situation.

You can experience emotions all over your body. It's common for many people who are stressed to experience neck tension, shoulder tightness, and headaches. This is the body communicating that you're spending too much time in your head, agonizing over long to-do lists or how to find the best way to address a problem.

While there are common trends of body cues, how you connect a feeling to a bodily cue is highly individual. There are no right or wrong answers, no standard to live up to—just the truths that your subconscious self, your shadow, is trying to get you to pay attention to.

Have you ever noticed a physical sensation when you simultaneously had an emotional reaction? What did you notice? What bodily cues come up for you?

As you sit and reflect in this moment, right now, what can you sense in your body? Do you notice any places of ease or tension? What might your body be trying to tell you about your current experience?

What practices do you currently have that you can build on to better understand your body and its clues to your shadow self?

AFFIRMATIONS

By paying attention to my body, I
can gain greater insight into what
my shadow self is reacting to.

Learning to interpret my own bodily cues helps
me better understand my feelings and desires.

Listening to my body is a new skill. I will
have patience as I make time to listen to it.

IDENTIFY YOUR TRIGGERS

Have you ever just been going about your business when suddenly you have an unexpected emotional reaction out of nowhere? If so, you experienced a trigger.

Socially, when we talk about triggers, we think of them as things that we want to avoid at all costs. But triggers are incredibly helpful sources of data for doing shadow work. They represent the small, and sometimes subtle, cues that you are reacting to some deep shadow material. When people say they are triggered, they typically mean that they have just experienced an emotional—and often simultaneous physical—reaction to something in their environment. That stimulating event (trigger) brought some difficult emotions to the surface. People often recognize that something has occurred, but perhaps they're not exactly sure what that specific trigger was or why it occurred.

Triggers almost always point to shadow material or past trauma that you've experienced. And this doesn't have to mean that the experience was earth-shattering for you—not all trauma is—but it means you were psychologically changed by that experience. Continuously responding to that same trigger, in the same way, is a sign that you require more healing.

The cues that lead to unwanted physical or emotional reactions can be large or quite subtle. For someone who has experienced a devastating car accident, for example, they might experience a rapid onset of anxiety when getting into a car. But what if the trigger is something more subtle, like a sharp comment from someone that you trust or a stranger not holding the door for you as you enter a building behind them? It can be harder to decipher what those moments trigger, especially if you don't clock them as meaningful bits of shadow material.

You can also experience triggers from a distance. Things that you read online can trigger emotional reactions and deep pain. This can cause you to react very strongly, particularly when you're already feeling on edge. For example, if mainstream society has told you repeatedly that because of your identities you're somehow less than others, a comment on social media on that topic can leave you feeling enraged and deeply hurt, as it reminds you of how society has deemed you intolerable or unacceptable. In this way, you can experience triggers even when you personally aren't the intended target. You can experience a trigger vicariously.

You cannot escape being triggered. It is not a personal failure to react to your environment, no matter how big or small. By taking time to identify and better understand your own triggers, you empower yourself to respond in ways that feel less disruptive for you moving forward. By exploring these triggers more deeply, you also make space to integrate your shadow side.

Think back to a time in which you felt an emotional or physical sensation out of nowhere. What came up for you and what do you think your body was trying to tell you? What stimuli were you reacting to?

What common signs (emotional and/or physical reactions) do you notice when something is bothering you?

If you are already aware of some of your common triggers, write each one down (no matter how small it may seem) and ask yourself, "What could this really be about? What makes each trigger so bothersome for me? What deeper points might they be striking?"

AFFIRMATIONS

Being triggered is not a personal failure.

My triggers provide me greater
clarity for my healing.

Avoiding my triggers only reinforces
them. I can approach them safely.

I can learn to respond to my triggers
in ways I can feel good about.

REACT TO DISAPPOINTMENT

It is never a good feeling to be staring down disappointment. When you have expectations for some event or person, and the experience doesn't quite live up to what you imagined, it can be devastating. This can also be a very enlightening time to better understand your shadow side.

Disappointment is an inevitable part of the human experience. You may experience this in large ways (like facing divorce or losing out on a job opportunity) or in much more mundane situations (like when a partner doesn't validate your feelings in the moment). In all situations, the pangs you feel represent the distance between your hopes and desires, and the reality that you are experiencing in that moment.

While experiencing disappointment isn't unique to any of us, your response to this experience can be incredibly unique and detailed. This is where you have the space to better understand yourself and unpack material that may be just outside of your normal day-to-day consciousness. Just like any other feeling, being disappointed is a valid experience on its own. You do not have to justify or rationalize this feeling in any way. You can, however, work to better understand your personal patterns through deeper exploration. This can give you greater insight into these hidden pain points and generate ideas for potential resolutions when these feelings come up again.

There is not one right way to process disappointment. However, how you respond to disappointment gives you much-needed data to investigate and analyze. Disappointment can lead you down a path of sadness. You may withdraw or isolate. You may even start to doubt yourself and the expectations you had for this person or situation. You might tend to lean into more outward expressions of anger and frustration when being let down. You might scold your partner or minimize a situation because "I didn't really care anyway!" We all have unique ways in which we respond to disappointment.

These visceral, and often automatic, responses are incredibly revealing. If you take a moment to reflect deeper, you can find yourself transported back to another time in your personal history when you were feeling similarly. Maybe you experienced that disappointment at the hands of a parent or another authority figure. Or perhaps you experienced your hopes and plans crashing at a pivotal time in your life. It's likely that you still have some unfinished business with those moments. You repress them to continue to function but may forget that your shadow self isn't as forgiving. The shadow doesn't simply forget—it just cloaks painful thoughts and memories until you can make the choice to consciously deal with them. Ask yourself: "Is that time right now?"

How do you typically respond to someone (or something) not meeting your expectations? How does disappointment manifest for you?

Do you think this reaction represents a pattern over time? If you start to think through your history, what disappointments (and reactions) immediately come up for you?

For those disappointing experiences, what do you think you need to address those situations now?

How can you integrate this new insight into your daily life?

AFFIRMATIONS

I do not need to rationalize or justify
my feelings of disappointment.

Disappointment represents the gap between
my expectations and my lived reality.

Through my shadow work, I can better
integrate my history with disappointment
and create new ways to respond.

EXPLORE YOUR BOUNDARIES

As mental health awareness becomes more mainstream, so have conversations around how we navigate boundaries and limits with the people around us. There is a lot of confusion about what boundaries are, what they mean, and how to set them well. This entry will give you more insight into boundaries and reflect on how you can apply them concretely in your life to better suit your needs.

We can't talk about boundaries without talking about the shadow. This is part of the conversation about boundaries that is often missing, yet the context is critical. Boundaries represent the distance at which you can provide care for yourself. At the center of boundary setting lies two very important themes: safety and self-care. Both are often central in shadow work.

Our brains tend to develop strategies, or patterns, to keep us emotionally safe. Depending on your own individual history, these patterns of response may also be rooted in historical traumas and repressed shadow material. For example, some people who experience trauma early on in childhood, especially relational trauma, feel safer with more interpersonal distance, or by practicing avoidance. Despite wanting closer relations, you may perceive intimate connections as dangerous and create regular distance between yourself and others. The old wounds, especially if unhealed, run the show. You can't believe that intimacy also means safety. To get closer to people and develop more intimate relationships, you would need to integrate the wounds of the shadow and learn to tolerate the anxiety of closeness. You would need to change your boundaries around intimacy to achieve this.

By contrast, it is not uncommon for those living with histories of physical or sexual abuse to rely on a pattern of fawning, or be perpetually acquiescent to the needs of others around them. If this sounds like you, then you likely often feel unfulfilled in your relationships. Because of a traumatic past, you believe that fawning is the only way to keep yourself safe or wanted. Over time, this pattern makes it difficult to listen to one's own needs and desires.

When you don't address these painful points hidden in your shadow side, you get stuck. You rely on certain boundaries and patterns to overcompensate for past pain. This can create other problems. The person who relies on distance will likely have extremely rigid boundaries with others in everyday life. Others in their life may often feel like they don't truly know this person well. By contrast, the person who tends to rely on fawning will likely have much more permeable boundaries, despite it continuously costing them peace of mind and creating codependency issues.

How do you feel about the boundaries you have in your relationships right now?

How might your boundaries be informed by your personal history?

When you think of themes like safety and protection, what thoughts immediately come up for you? Do you notice any patterns in those thoughts and feelings over time?

AFFIRMATIONS

I use boundaries to care for
myself and find safety.

I can learn to adjust my boundaries to protect
myself and have connection with others.

My boundaries help me take care
of my mind, body, and spirit.

ENGAGE THE SIX TYPES OF BOUNDARIES

In the previous exercise you learned that boundaries are complex and informed by your personal history. It's important to know that we tend to engage with boundaries from six main categories: emotional, intellectual, material, physical, sexual, and time.

- **Emotional boundaries refer to the sharing of emotional content and information.** Think of with whom and how often you share your honest feelings. It is common to have more permeable (porous) emotional boundaries with those who are intimately connected to you (your partner and loved ones, for example) and more rigid boundaries with professional contacts like work colleagues or business partners who are not also friends.
- **Intellectual boundaries refer to the sharing of thoughts and ideas.** Do you often feel respected when you share your thoughts and opinions with others? If not, you may want to think about healthier (or more rigid) boundaries with certain people, or in certain contexts.
- **Material boundaries refer to the extent by which you share your resources and goods with those around you.** This could refer to lending out/borrowing physical things like food, clothing, books, or money, but could also refer to more abstract things like access to other social or professional contacts.

- **Physical boundaries refer to how much access someone has to your body or personal environment.** For instance, you may consider yourself "a hugger" if you have more flexible physical boundaries, but might have more rigid boundaries in this area if you prefer not to shake hands with people you meet.
- **Sexual boundaries refer to the limits and guidelines for how you express your sexual identity and sexuality.** This can refer to the verbal sharing of personal information about how you identify or the things that you enjoy sexually, all the way to the extent to which you engage in physical acts with another person (which could differ with a committed versus casual sexual partner, for example).
- **Time boundaries refer to how you may choose to spend your time.** People with more rigid time boundaries might allot for only specific times for meetings, phone calls, and so on, while someone with more porous boundaries might find themselves often running out of time as they do not intentionally set time limits with themselves and others. You may also have different boundaries with how you spend your time with different groups of people (family members, friends, romantic partners, coworkers, and so on).

As you get deeper into the work on boundaries, you may feel compelled to consider rigid or porous boundaries as all bad, but that's not exactly the case. "Healthy" boundaries (or the ones that are best for you) may look rigid or much more porous depending on your life's circumstances. For instance, you might have much more rigid boundaries with an abusive ex-partner with whom you share parental rights but might have more emotionally porous boundaries with your ex's mother as a source of emotional support.

When it comes to boundaries, your typical patterns tend to reveal buried shadow material, often as it relates to experiences that your inner child experienced during formative years. Loss, safety, security, and negligence are all themes that play a role in how you conceptualize boundaries as an adult and what healthy boundaries look like. Take some time to do an audit of your personal boundaries and you will likely learn a lot about shadow material that stays just out of your awareness most days.

What boundary category are you most often conscious of and effective at managing? Which categories do you feel most insecure about?

What shadow material may be informing your difficulty in setting healthier boundaries? What experiences or principles inform your difficulty?

Take a moment to consider how you can work on developing healthier boundaries. What steps do you need to take to move forward, and what resources can help you along the way?

AFFIRMATIONS

Boundaries are a tool to use to care for
myself and to feel safe and secure.

It is my right to choose appropriate boundaries
for my specific circumstances moving forward.

I can honor the boundaries of others around
me so that they can feel safe too.

REFLECT ON UNINTENDED ACTIONS

It is important to be mindful of your actions and choices. When you develop a practice of mindful self-awareness, you ensure that you live your life in ways that feel good for you and utilize the full benefits of the environments you find yourself in. However, sometimes you also make mistakes and take actions that you look back on with guilt and shame.

You might say, "I didn't mean to do that!" when you reflect on a personal mistake. Typically, this realization strikes when someone you have offended is thoughtful enough to share their experience of your behavior. Receiving this kind of feedback can be hard. It can be both an intellectual and an emotional injury.

Most of us like to think of ourselves as self-aware and intentional beings and many of us are! The reality is, however, that when mired down with long days and a complex daily life, your nervous system simply doesn't have the space or capacity to process every action or choice that you make. When things do not go quite the way you intended, your shadow self can easily be surprised, activated, and triggered.

If you've ever been in a situation when a loved one has shared their feelings about something you did, then you know this feeling. The feedback triggered some negative thoughts or self-doubt about yourself. You might have immediately fallen on the proverbial sword and apologized profusely. You might even be shocked by their feedback, as you hadn't yet considered how your actions impacted them. It's common to react defensively as you seek to protect your ego and reputation. In any of those circumstances, the feedback you received likely struck a deep part of you.

You might have also experienced a personal crisis when the situation was high stakes, like making a mistake at work on an important project or hurting your partner's feelings. These moments can derail you, especially when that feedback comes from someone you love and care about.

To better understand your shadow self, you must look beyond the action itself and pay attention to both impact and intention. Mistakes are not intentional, so then why do you feel shame and guilt around them? Most likely because your unintended action (the mistake) represents something deeper within yourself. Maybe you feel ongoing pressure to be perfect and see this mistake as a crack in that perfect veneer. Or perhaps you thought you made a choice that aligned with your values but that ended up disrupting someone else's experience. This might remind you of your own self-centered impulses you strive to avoid. How you respond to these moments, and what you feel, points to the long-held scripts that reside within your shadow self. This is an opportunity to dig deeper and learn more about who you are, and the inspiration behind the choices you make.

Think of a recent time in which you thought you acted out of character or in an unexpected way. What happened? What were the circumstances surrounding that behavior?

Then start to look at your behavior through a more curious, rather than a judgmental, lens. What do you think you were hoping to achieve with your action(s)? Assume that your actions weren't intentional or malicious—what do you think you stood to gain from taking the actions you did?

Does this give you any further insight into shadow material you weren't immediately aware of at that moment?

How can you go about addressing those actions now? Are there opportunities to make amends or to practice self-compassion?

AFFIRMATIONS

It is okay for me to make mistakes.

I can feel guilty for making a misstep, but I do not need to punish myself for acting in self-interest.

I can move forward as I integrate the lessons learned and strike a balance between meeting my needs and respecting those around me.

DEAL WITH CONFLICT

Conflict and confrontation are similar concepts. As you think about confrontation, you might think of what it means to bring your concerns to someone after they've done something to upset you. You may have been wronged or personally offended by their behavior and need to assert yourself to address the issue. Confrontation is often a more immediate response to a specific situation.

By contrast, conflict can be either situational or about something that's more long-standing. For instance, you find yourself in a romantic relationship that's often plagued by regular arguing and other difficulties. In that environment you may not need to confront your partner but may be living in constant conflict. This can be incredibly difficult and bring up shadow material.

Your relationship to conflict is influenced by your history, and some past experiences may have been pushed to the more subconscious parts of your psyche. If you grew up in an abusive household, or experienced an abusive relationship as an adult, then you may consciously try to avoid similar dynamics in the future. But, if you've found yourself in a similar dynamic in your adult life, then it's likely that shadow material is trying to create an opportunity to resolve past hurt.

Alternatively, feelings of insecurity or low self-worth might cause you to avoid necessary conflict and problem solving. This may be because you feel like you can't, or shouldn't, resolve whatever issue lies in front of you.

On a basic level, it's important to note that conflict is difficult and can be quite draining. This might lead you to consistently doubt your ability to navigate, and survive, conflict when it does knock on your doorstep. Take a moment to explore your experiences with conflict and resolution with the questions that follow.

Think about a period in your life when you felt like you were "in conflict" with someone. As you reimagine that time right now, what feelings or sensations come up for you? Can you map those sensations on your body?

What role has conflict played throughout your history? Are there any moments within your family of origin, friend group, or romantic relationship that come up for you as significant?

How do you think these previous experiences have impacted you and how you respond to conflict? What parts do you think have become a part of your shadow self?

AFFIRMATIONS

I am doing my best to better
respond to conflict in my life.

I can use my voice to stick up for myself
and take action to work through conflict.

I empower myself to address conflict with
more courage and resolve in the future.

EXPLORE BEING BUSY

Stay busy. Be productive. Find the best ways to optimize your time and energy. Try this scheduling tool! Minimize distraction with these tips and you'll get it all done!

Does any of this sound familiar to you? It seems like these days we all have an internal dialogue pushing us to be more productive, to achieve more, and just keep working. You push yourself to send that last email or check off the next thing on your to-do list. Maybe you feel accomplished when you finally decide to stop for a moment, or maybe you only see all the other things that you still need to do and feel down, hopeless, or worthless.

Being busy, however, doesn't just refer to things that are traditionally productive, like work and other assignments. Filling your schedule to the brim with exercising or social events to the point of emotional or physical exhaustion also isn't unheard of. You must keep busy. You must keep moving forward. But why?

Maybe you find yourself using the language of being busy in your conversations with others: "I'm just so busy these days!" "I don't know if I'll have the time." These are common phrases to throw around these days, but what does being busy really mean for you?

Perhaps you see being busy as a sign of status or achievement (busy people get things done and make more money) or maybe you often find yourself pressured to achieve more (if you don't do more, maybe something is wrong with you). What might the more unconscious part of you be trying to communicate as you dash from appointment to meeting to social event to task and chore? What are you missing?

When we think of the shadow parts of ourselves, we tend to think of the negative thoughts and feelings—the abysmal parts of our psyches. But when we think of being busy we (collectively) brandish our fervor like a badge of honor. If being busy means existing in the light of productivity, then does not being busy mean being enveloped by the darkness of the shadow? What happens then?

For many, being busy often means doing good...maybe even being good. Could that be true for you? Sure, having things to do and responsibilities to take care of can be great, but what if being busy is also a cloak for some other truths you try to avoid?

In what ways do you buy into or appreciate hustle culture? How do you know when you've done enough? Where is the line between being too busy and productive enough?

What happens when you aren't so busy? Are there any thoughts or feelings that tend to come up for you? What might your shadow be trying to reveal to you?

In what ways does being busy make you visible? In what ways might it help you hide?

Could staying busy keep you from leaning into treating yourself with care and softness? What hidden material might be influencing that way of thinking?

AFFIRMATIONS

Being busy does not make me more worthy.

I am good, whole, and worthy just as I am.

I can take time to experience joy,
outside of accomplishment.

LEARN ABOUT ATTACHMENT STYLE THEORY

Just as shadow work often involves exploring the inner child, attachment theory also often comes up as you seek a better understanding of yourself and how you navigate relationships. Attachment theory can provide you with a foundation to better understand how and why you respond in the ways that you do while in relationships. Attachment theory is not a perfect theory, and social scientists have legitimate questions about its application to adult romantic relationships. Even so, it can offer a foundation by which to continue personal exploration.

Attachment theory was popularized by psychoanalyst John Bowlby. He wanted to better understand the why behind our feelings of closeness and intimacy to those around us. His work focused on the relationship between the primary caregiver (often a biological mother) and child. In his early work, and in the work of his predecessors on human connection, attachment was viewed as an evolutionary process by which infants and children could guarantee survival. That is, early theories centered on the idea that our attachment with a mother was solely due to their ability to provide physical sustenance (milk) and physical protection for survival. As the study of attachment grew, a new theory appeared—those bonds aren't just formed due to basic needs of survival, but are also heavily influenced by psychological and emotional nurturance. That is, later theories stated that we feel attached and connected to parents who are responsive to our emotional needs, as well as our physical ones. This was demonstrated by the experiments of psychologist Mary Ainsworth in the 1970s.

These early findings helped create three basic attachment styles: secure, ambivalent-insecure (anxious), and avoidant-insecure (dismissive-avoidant). Later research introduced the disorganized-insecure (fearful-avoidant) type. If you are not familiar with the research in this area, you can learn more in Appendix B.

Now, take a moment to consider the inner child work that you've been doing so far. Have any themes come up with respect to feeling safe and/or having (or not having) your needs met? If so, it's likely you are uncovering repressed feelings that you couldn't honor and locate as a child. When you get clearer on those experiences and needs you had as a child, you gain insight into your attachment style and discover tender spots in need of healing.

Take a moment to reflect on these attachment styles and inner child work you've done so far. Have any themes come up of safety/lack of safety in relationships? What style sounds the most like you? Do you often seek out relationships or avoid them? Do you feel confused or anxious most of the time or calm and confident (especially in the early stages of making a connection)?

What previous experiences start to come up for you when you think about how your primary caregivers, or parents, responded to your needs?

What other attachment injuries did you experience (but perhaps forget) as you started to seek out romantic and intimate relationships as a teen and young adult? How did those relationships feel for you?

AFFIRMATIONS

My experiences in early childhood
are powerful but do not have to
dictate my future relationships.

I can work to address, and attend to,
attachment injuries I've experienced
through my shadow work.

I have the capacity to heal in deep
connection with myself and others.

REPARENT YOUR INNER CHILD

As you may have gathered from several of the previous entries, inner child exploration is often a very important part of shadow work. A significant portion of work that you encounter with shadow material connects to early life experiences because in your younger years you often lean on repression and aren't as dynamic in making sense of the world around you. Now that you've been able to establish contact with the inner child, you can take the next step and begin exploring what it might be like to reparent that inner child.

Reparenting is the process by which you learn to nurture and nourish your inner child. It rests on the idea that as a more evolved adult (with greater self-awareness and language) you can fill in some of the gaps that your primary caregivers may not have tended to as well in your younger years. Reparenting is establishing a loving relationship with your inner child and extending to them the kind of love and kindness that you feel you still need. This work is not an indictment on parenting. It's an act of self-love seeking to fill in those subjective gaps that you may feel while looking back on your younger years.

It can be difficult for most generally self-aware adults to connect deeply to their inner child. The ego tends to get in the way and tells you that inner child work is silly, or that you are just being "dramatic." Sometimes it is dramatic; sometimes it may feel silly—but that doesn't make the feelings you have any less true, or in any less need of healing.

The inner child rests within the shadow, normally just outside of daily consciousness. It becomes activated when triggered. The inner child can be boisterous, needy, or even aggressive and manipulative. The inner child tends to act and need impulsively, without regard for the needs of others. When triggered, the inner child seeks support, care, and safety. Now, as an adult, you have greater capacity to give your inner child what they need.

When it comes to doing the work of reparenting, it is likely that you will find yourself rejecting all these selfish, needy tendencies. Trust that you can, and will, successfully find ways to negotiate being in touch with your inner child and listening to their needs, while also integrating them into your daily life alongside the people you care about most. Caring for yourself and your needs is not selfish...it is necessary. Giving your inner child the attention and care they need is loving and healing yourself. Allow yourself to pay attention to this inner child when they become activated and agitated, as you the observer take notice of rising shadow material.

Questions for Reflection

How do you think your parents fared in providing the kind of care and attention that you needed? What care gaps did you notice then and what wounds remain?

Most of us have core stories or scripts that become activated in inner child work, like "No one cares about how I feel." What scripts come up for you often now? Take a moment to consider how those stories might be your inner child talking.

Reparenting activities might often look like doing things that kids normally do when upset, like taking a time out, engaging in some pleasurable activity, asking for a hug, and so on. What are some options that you can begin to use to reparent your inner child? List some ideas in the area that follows.

AFFIRMATIONS

My inner child becomes activated when I find
myself triggered in everyday situations.

Caring for myself, and my needs, is
not selfish. It is necessary.

If I take time to communicate with my inner
child, I can take better care of myself and heal.

ADDRESS LONELINESS

As you may have gathered from the previous exercises in this book, shadow work often means leaning into uncomfortable emotions, working to understand them more fully, and creating space for them in our lives. This is also true for addressing loneliness.

Being physically alone and feeling alone are two very different experiences. The first is a physical state of being—an observation that there is no one around you. The latter represents a feeling of being disconnected from others in the world around you, almost as if you're moving through your life alone. This feeling is difficult to create space for, as it can be painful and frightening. It's a big, existential feeling.

In one way, you are always alone. Only you can completely understand the workings of your internal world, and many struggle to do that. This struggle is common, and therefore you may seek out opportunities for deeper self-reflection, like within the pages of this book. You may also try to see yourself reflected in poems, stories, and other works of art. These things help you connect to yourself as well as to other people and the collective consciousness. This brings connection, and helps you cope with the experience of feeling alone.

Existential aloneness often feels too big and too vast to hold on to. Maybe you think that if you allow space for it in your life then it will be too painful. Perhaps if you acknowledge how alone you are then you won't be able to recover. Life could feel meaningless and even more difficult to cope with.

The irony, however, is that in another way you are truly never alone. You can obviously be physically alone in a space. You can be without parents, family, or loved ones, but this kind of aloneness isn't eternal. Even if you are alone now, you also have experiences in which you felt a meaningful connection with another being (whether that be human or animal). Relationships can, of course, be unfulfilling and troubled, but we all have experiences in which we were connected to someone—whether it was good or bad. Rarely are relationships either one or the other; they are usually some complex dynamic of both joyous and devastating. You always have connection within these memories.

You also have access to connection in other places. You have memories and connections to characters in art that can remind you of what it's like to be—and feel—truly human and connected.

Despite this, there are times you may feel alone. It can almost be unbearable and hard to cope. You may dull the feeling with substances or other strategies that aren't as healthy for you, but what if you could allow yourself to connect to that feeling of aloneness and honor the depth of that shadow? Could that acknowledgment bring about some new ease or understanding about the meaning of connection in your life?

Have you ever experienced what it is to feel alone? What was that like for you and how did you cope?

What things or people in your life (present or past) have helped you feel less alone?

What steps can you take moving forward to respond when you begin to feel alone or disconnected?

AFFIRMATIONS

Being alone and feeling alone are
two different experiences.

It is normal to sometimes feel alone,
even when I'm not physically alone.

Being alone is a normal part of being
human. When I feel alone I can revisit
past connections, discover new meaning,
and foster connection with others.

TAKE A LOOK AT SEXUAL INTIMACY

In addition to darker thoughts and feelings like rage, anger, depression, and shame, socially taboo subjects like sex and sexuality often find themselves hidden in the recesses of our shadow selves. Every culture has its own understanding and view of what sexual intimacy is and what it represents. The standards of each society around sexual intimacy are often well known within the community. These messages and standards become a part of our lives, particularly as we begin to grow toward, and beyond, puberty. Parents and other authority figures (such as religious figures and educators) are most often our primary messengers about what sex and sexuality means, and we also receive supplemental information from peers and other sources like the media.

Some cultures see sexual intimacy as solely a means to a reproductive end, while others consider a wider range of possibilities for sex and desire. Irrespective of which culture you come from, it is not uncommon for many people to have sex/sexuality represented, in some part, within their shadows. Sex-shaming has existed throughout history in various forms.

Sexual intimacy and sexuality have long been policed throughout cultures and history, despite the well-documented history of the existence of a variety of sexual identities, activities, and desires. If you live in a more socially repressed society, then the feedback and shaming around sexuality can start young and be particularly strong.

Being educated about your body, how it works, and your relationship to desire and fantasy is all a part of sexual intimacy and sexuality. However, it is relatively uncommon for people (especially in North America, but in other parts of the world as well) to get a full exploration of what it means to desire and be desired sexually. This often means that sexual intimacy becomes a hush-hush topic.

While the message is indirect, it is clear. Sexual intimacy and sexuality are things that you shouldn't talk about at all, or should only be talked about in very specific, private circumstances and situations. Sexuality, according to this philosophy, should be repressed. You are only allowed to have conversations about sex with the one partner you're socially allowed to crave. Your sexuality must exist within the most private parts of yourself. You must enjoy your sexuality, but only in the dark, both literally and figuratively.

This kind of relationship with sexuality creates shame. It can make you think of yourself as bad for having any sexual desires. And every time you act (or even think about acting) on these taboo impulses, you feel guilt. This can create a relationship with sex and sexuality that is more complicated and messier than it needs to be.

If you create some space to see yourself and your desires more freely through shadow integration, then you can begin to reduce the silence and shame. You can experience greater freedom within your desires whether you choose to act on them or not. Through shadow work, you get to develop and accept yourself as a normal, sexual being.

What messages have you heard throughout your life about sexual intimacy and sexuality? Were those messages expansive and encouraging? Or restrictive and limiting?

How would you describe your current relationship to sexual intimacy?

What interests or desires do you have that feel too threatening or abnormal to share with someone else?

How can you begin to cultivate self-compassion for your desires and fantasies (whether you act on them or not)?

AFFIRMATIONS

My sexuality is mine, and mine alone.

My desires can exist without fear or shame.

I can make space for my feelings and fantasies whether I choose to act on them or not.

EXPLORE CREATIVITY

While we often talk about the shadow side as the respite for all things dark and unsightly, it is also responsible for housing beautiful parts of yourself. The depth of feeling that exists within the shadow means that it is also ripe with beautiful, creative potential.

Sublimation, as Sigmund Freud described, is a defense mechanism by which we turn unacceptable thoughts and feelings into more socially appropriate activities and ways of coping. Sublimation requires you to be creative. This might go beyond the typical ways you might think of creativity (like creative and expressive arts). Given sublimation's particular brand of alchemy, it's easy to see the connection with shadow work. While much of how you learn to cope with shadow material can involve avoidance and repression, it can also be creative and transformative.

It's not uncommon for musicians to turn memories of painful relationships, and other dark times in their life, into beautiful songs. Sometimes those songs are full of rage and obvious heartbreak. These are examples of sublimating deep relational pain into accessible, relatable beauty that the rest of the world also gets to enjoy.

But you don't need to be an award-winning musician or otherwise creative person to embrace sublimation and creativity. Everyone relies on sublimation in a variety of ways, which means that you also have access to creativity. This creativity can be a means to access deeper, subconscious thoughts and feelings.

Think about the last time that you felt very angry at someone. Let's say you were driving in traffic and encountered a reckless driver who put you at risk for a traffic accident. You, of course, felt angry. But, instead of getting out of your car and resorting to a fistfight, or running the other car off the road, perhaps you cussed aloud to yourself and turned on intense music to scream-sing along to to lean into your rage. This is a creative solution to managing overwhelming anger and frustration. You get to act out, and express, your anger without causing any actual harm to yourself or others. This is sublimation.

Alternatively, maybe you've just experienced a vicious battle with cancer. You take some time to process all your own feelings, but then you turn your energy toward creating more spaces for other cancer patients to thrive and heal. You use your pain and experience to fuel support and care for others. This is sublimation too.

Both are examples of the creativity that everyone has inside. We are all born natural creators if we allow ourselves to be. Some people hold on to their ability to consciously create, but many begin to get rewarded for other pursuits (which you may even like a great deal). As a result, you stop seeing yourself as a creative being as you age. You forget that you are always creating. Creativity and sublimation are great ways that you can access shadow material, whether that creativity is solely for self-benefit or if it provides art for the people around you to enjoy.

If you revisit memories of your childhood, what were your favorite ways to create or embrace your imagination?

Do you see the ways in which you are still a creative being in your life currently?

What ways might sublimation be showing up in your life to help you cope with challenging life circumstances or experiences?

How do you think you can more consciously incorporate creativity (or even play) in your life moving forward? In what forms could this revised perspective on creativity be accessible for you?

AFFIRMATIONS

All humans are imaginative beings
with the capacity to create.

We often create by sublimating and turning a
negative experience into a more positive one.

I do not have to place self-imposed
limits on myself, or my creativity.

EXAMINE INSECURITY

Everyone has at least one part of themselves that they don't like. We all have insecurities. You might be insecure about your looks. You might experience guilt or shame around previous sexual experiences. You could be struggling to reach new levels of success in your work life because you don't think you can rise to the challenge.

It is likely that you may also be dealing with more than one insecurity, in more than one area. Many people do! As you may have gathered from other sections in this book, what exists in the shadow is often the result of internalizing the message that there are things inside you that you need to repress, or hide, to be acceptable. This can apply to your more superficial self (outward appearance), as well as deeper parts of yourself (like how you navigate relationships or perform at work).

You may find that you work very hard to hide the less desirable parts of yourself to others. You may hide your insecurities to make sure that you're keeping up with the other people around you. You want others to see you as good enough, worthy enough, even if you can't be convinced of your own worthiness. The ironic part is, you work very hard to shield your insecurities from others while they are also doing the same. This creates a more controlled, superficial dynamic within relationships. The insecurities make you desperate to avoid truly being seen, while still desiring to be completely seen and accepted.

When you internalize these distorted images of yourself, you can become hyper-focused on the ways in which you think you are inadequate. A crooked smile becomes evidence of just how unattractive you are. A painful relationship history means you are damaged goods to anyone new. Being too big for a sample size means you don't deserve to feel beautiful. As a result, you work very hard in your relationships to hide your insecurities and points of pain. You may act from a place of superficiality so as to not allow anyone, or even yourself, to acknowledge the realities of your shadow self. You simultaneously want to be seen and accepted, yet you regularly participate in your own hiding to avoid experiencing further judgment and psychological damage. This hiding is simultaneously self-protecting and self-abusive, as you communicate to yourself how unworthy you are of truly being seen. You deserve better than this.

This hiding can be somewhat effective even if it is not sustainable. Denying or hiding your insecurities allows you to emotionally bypass them. You build emotional walls that tell the rest of the world, "No, I'm good, really!" when you are struggling. Those insecurities become a burdensome cross to bear. Eventually, they seep deeper into your subconscious and allow you to convince yourself of your own delusions with personal satisfaction. This works, albeit temporarily, until some unanticipated situation comes up and reactivates these shadow insecurities, disrupting the artifice you've created for yourself. Then you're faced with those insecurities all over again.

But, if you consciously make space for them, you can learn to live alongside your insecurities with compassion.

How does insecurity tend to show up in your life? What behaviors or actions do you think might be brought on by your personal insecurities?

What situations from your past do you think have created/ impacted this insecurity? How might they be connected?

What areas of life (work, school, romantic relationships, and so on) allow your insecurities to come up most often?

Are there opportunities for further healing and self-acceptance that you're now beginning to consider? How might you offer more kindness to yourself for your insecurities?

AFFIRMATIONS

I can be unhappy with a part of myself and still be worthy of love, care, and compassion.

My insecurities are dictated by my past. I will work to minimize their impact on my future.

My pain points and insecurities are opportunities for growth and healing.

PROCESS LOSS

Grief and loss are normal parts of life. Yet, we don't always treat these experiences and the related feelings as normal and acceptable. It is this rejection that makes processing loss necessary for doing shadow work.

It's not uncommon for grief and loss to come up multiple times while doing shadow work. As you grow throughout life, you may experience multiple losses. As you age you may experience the loss of a person you loved deeply or a family pet and it can be difficult to cope with that loss. But you also likely lived through other important losses such as the loss of a relationship, the loss of innocence, missing out on a specific event or experience you thought you would have, or even the loss of a physical item that held significant meaning. While each of these examples may not feel the same, each of these experiences can be painful and profound. You may know this, yet you don't make enough space to connect to these feelings of loss. Sometimes we avoid these feelings because we fear that experiencing them will be too much, or because we've learned that processing loss must look a certain way, or adhere to an unrealistic timeline determined by social, and cultural, standards.

You see conversations about loss happening every day in the news and online. You may also have conversations about loss in therapy or in spiritual and religious spaces. Even in these spaces, you may minimize the impact of loss in your life through intellectualization and relying on spiritual clichés. You unintentionally invalidate the pain of each loss as you try to continue living your life.

You are told that, at some point, you should be well enough to put the pain and hurt of loss behind you and move on, simply because that's what "healthy" people do. Even the professional mental health field limits the amount of time that is reasonable to grieve a loss—turning the natural experience of lifelong grief into a diagnosis of dysfunction.

As a result, it is common to either feel loss very briefly and move on, or to deny that it has even really moved you emotionally at all. With the pressure to perform that you "coped with" the loss, your real feelings about it are banished to the shadow, often resurfacing only when triggered by happenstance. You see a movie or hear a song that reminds you of who or what you've lost. Even if you allow yourself this brief dip into mourning, you might silently wipe away your tears and go about your daily life. At other times you may be brave enough to show up fully in your grief, only to receive feedback that it's too much. Then, you retreat. The grief shrinks back into the shadow.

You can learn to live with loss and the feelings that come along with it. You don't have to relegate your feelings of grief just to angel anniversaries or memorial services. You can create space to live alongside loss, knowing it has helped inform who you are and how you will live moving forward.

What messages have you received in your life about how to cope with loss? What have you observed in your life, growing up and until now as an adult, about what it means to process loss and grief?

Are there any losses from your life that you've found difficult to create space for? What/who are they? How does it feel for you when you start to reconnect with those moments?

What might you want, or need, to support your effort in living alongside grief?

AFFIRMATIONS

Loss is a normal, and inevitable,
part of the human experience.

There is no right timeline for
processing my grief and loss.

I can learn to live with my loss.

EXPLORE THE MEANINGS OF SYMBOLS

As you likely have gathered by now, accessing the shadow self often means finding creative ways to unlock the hidden parts of yourself. You can do this through exercises that focus on things such as mindful reflection, the inner child, and dream analysis. You may need to use symbols (both in dreams and otherwise) to help you continue to develop greater insight into what most often lies just out of your conscious mind.

Symbols are a big part of traditional psychoanalytic work for this reason. Theoretically, the subconscious (shadow) material that is too difficult to face head-on comes to your conscious mind in the form of symbols and hidden meanings. As a result, analyzing dreams can often feel like a combination of a scavenger hunt and logic puzzle all rolled into one. Symbols can help you decode these messages.

There are both personal and collective symbols that you should consider in shadow work. Personal symbols might be themes, or motifs, that you've noticed come up often in your life. Chances are that these symbols have deep personal meaning. They might have entered your life during a specific experience (like being gifted a figurine for a holiday) and later take on more meaning. For instance, you might find yourself collecting (and being gifted) ceramic elephants over the years without much thought. But what might those elephants represent to you?

There are also common collective symbols that have roots in analysis and meaning throughout history. Darkness and light are symbols that we have collectively decided reference the evil and good in the world, respectively. This simple idea creates a connection that the shadow is some ominous creature that needs to be avoided. By contrast, we think about finding peace and redemption by ideas like "walking into the light" or "wearing the white hat." We attach meaning to symbols and they continue to inform our perspective.

You can argue the validity of other symbols from analytic theory; however, it's more important to assume that you have, at least to some extent, internalized them as your own. Sigmund Freud is usually cited as the creator of these symbols. His work often centered on psychosexual development, and therefore common universal symbols were the sword or stick representing a phallus/penis, a cave or house representing a vagina, and so forth.

Contemporary dream analysis goes beyond these and, I think, has a more comprehensive approach to symbol analysis. For example, a house may represent safety and security. If a home shows up in a dream, the state of that house could represent the extent to which you feel safe and secure in your waking life. A pristine, well-structured house might indicate stability, while a house with a crumbling foundation might mean that you think there is something deeply wrong in your life that needs your attention. Other universal symbols are death representing a dramatic life change or shift and nudity representing feeling emotionally vulnerable or exposed.

I've provided a few examples of symbols in this entry. What other general or mainstream symbols have you heard of frequently? And what are they meant to represent?

Are there any symbols or themes that come up in your dreams (or even in waking life often)?

What traits or ideas might this symbol represent for you? How might it be connected to your previous experiences and personal story?

AFFIRMATIONS

Each symbol I encounter offers insight
into my unconscious self.

Symbols can be both literal and figurative. I can
listen to my intuition as I explore the meaning for me.

I will explore symbols with
curiosity and non-judgment.

Symbol analysis can be confusing.
I don't need to find the "perfect" meaning
for my exploration to be valuable.

RECOVER FROM A MISSED OPPORTUNITY

Whenever you experience a disappointment, such as a missed opportunity, it can trigger a lot of negative thoughts and feelings. Some of these reactions are typical, like wishing that you still had the chance to take advantage of the opportunity, while others can be more insidious.

It's not uncommon for a missed opportunity to bring up shadow material. Feeling disappointment can often be a powerful catalyst for deeper thoughts and feelings to make their way to the surface. Such shadow material might represent negative thoughts about oneself (such as a lack of deservedness or general unworthiness, stupidity, and so on) or reflect on the difficulty in trusting others, or the universe, to come through for you.

You may rationally understand that you do not have access to every experience that you want. Yet, missing out on something that you believed you would, or could, have can be profoundly difficult to cope with. Maybe it's because your inner child has long wished for just that thing to come true. It's also common to experience regret for not acting sooner to go after what you want. This all can make it difficult to accept your own role in missing out on an opportunity. Your psyche comes to your defense, rationalizing away your hesitancy, often citing the real-world circumstances that stood in your way.

It is when you struggle to accept the reality of the missed opportunity that shadow material disrupts your mental health and sense of self. When your thoughts and feelings go beyond typical and mild feelings of disappointment, they can take on some other meaning. That means there may be unconscious material that requires your attention. The tinge of regret invites you to take a bit of a closer look at yourself in this kind of situation. But most often, either you may find yourself relying on external circumstances to cope with your behavior and the outcome, or you fall into depression seeing this event as evidence of how messed up you really are. But the truth is rarely that simple.

Each of these thought patterns has roots in your own personal history. The ways in which you respond reveal a lot about who you are, how you see yourself, and what parts of you still need healing and attention.

Think back to a time when you were faced with a missed opportunity. What feelings, other than disappointment, came up for you? Did those feelings seem proportional to that moment, or did they represent something bigger and broader?

If you take a moment to dig deeper, what thoughts about yourself (and/or those around you) come up as you reflect on a missed opportunity? What themes or scripts sound familiar to you?

What might those scripts be telling you about what rests in your shadow self? Is there some opportunity for integration, self-compassion, or healing?

What typically keeps you from acting on an opportunity that you're otherwise interested in?

AFFIRMATIONS

It's okay to feel sadness or disappointment
when facing a missed opportunity.

Feeling regret provides me with
an opportunity for more personal
understanding and self-compassion.

Even if I make a mistake, I am still
worthy of grace and compassion.

INTERACT WITH DIFFICULT PEOPLE

At one point or another we all come across difficult people in our lives. Whether this person is just annoying or more insidious in their behavior, there is almost always further insight we can gain from paying attention to how this person resonates within us.

You are sometimes forced to interact with people that you might otherwise avoid. These people can be your colleagues or coworkers (maybe more often a boss), but they might also be people you encounter by coincidence in life, like cashiers in a store or strangers on the street. You might push these people off into the "bad" category and vent to other friends or loved ones about that person who left you feeling out of sorts. You could throw out these experiences as small incidental moments, but you can also use these interactions to further your personal development and shadow integration.

For every reaction that you have in response to the people you encounter, there is more that you can learn about yourself. Not only is repression a common defense against the dark realities of your shadow self, but so is projection. Projection is the process by which you place your negative feelings, thoughts, and ideas onto another person. In shadow work this often means highlighting someone else's difficult and manipulative tendencies so that you do not have to address your own. This often causes splitting, or black-and-white thinking, where you conceptualize someone as only good or only bad. Of course, this is incredibly reductive and ignores the reality that we are all capable of being difficult, or toxic, in our own ways.

This is not to say that there are not categorically difficult, or harmful, people in the world. But even with those very difficult people, you have something to learn about yourself. Your distaste for them may also represent your refusal to see the ways in which you are like them—the ways in which you have capacity to be harmful and manipulative. Often, the most extreme and harmful people act out their shadow selves unconsciously on others—creating a trail of victims in their path as they refuse to heal their hidden wounds.

For most well-adjusted people, annoying or problematic behaviors only come in moments of great stress and don't cross a line. You likely do not categorically and systematically enact a pattern of harmful, toxic behaviors. However, it's important to recognize that you can also be difficult. You can play on someone's emotions to get what you want (be manipulative). You have the capacity to lie and cheat, even if this happens mostly in small ways that do not have much lasting impact.

By taking a deeper look inward, you can find clarity on why difficult people are so threatening to you. Perhaps they reflect your own darker impulses or moments in which you've been subjected to bad behavior from someone just like them. If you become familiar with the shadow parts of you that show up in these people, you can make peace with these darker parts of yourself and manage your responses to the people you encounter in everyday life. This kind of introspection also offers you the opportunity to offer yourself the compassion and acceptance that you need more of.

Questions for Reflection

What qualities have you observed in others that you often find most difficult? Take a moment to write down a few adjectives to capture them. Now, take a moment and look at the corresponding opposite adjectives from that list (for example: annoying turns into "pleasant to be around" in your second list). Does this new list represent the traits that you believe you demonstrate most, or want to portray most? Be honest.

When you encounter a difficult person, how does that feel for you? Do you notice any typical bodily or emotional responses at that moment?

Who are your core "difficult" people from your history? What experiences with these people do you still carry with you?

AFFIRMATIONS

I have the capacity to be difficult and
harmful at times (just like everyone else).

★

Being difficult does not mean I
am a villain or an abuser.

★

I can make space for my own personal
faults and difficulties. This will help me
better manage them and limit harm.

IDENTIFY TOXIC TRAITS

These days it seems like the word "toxic" has become a pop psychology buzzword. It is easier than ever to label someone's behavior as toxic. This often provides us with an opportunity to disparage the other and relegate them to the margins of society. In certain extreme situations, this kind of exile might be warranted. But this kind of categorization is often only moderately productive and, ironically, obscures another universal truth: We (humans) all have the capacity to be toxic. We all have "toxic" traits.

The shadow self is the Pandora's box of so many things, including the negative parts of yourself that you would much rather avoid. Sometimes these parts are relatively benign concerns, and at other times these parts are darker, more toxic traits that (most of the time) only show up incidentally. The toxic behaviors that come from this space are not malicious or intentional. Moreover, they are often misguided attempts to address some deeply unmet need. This could be long-standing frustrations about how others treat and interact with you, or repressed traumas that you've yet to more fully address and process.

It is much easier to cast out others who display these kinds of toxic traits than work through your own stuff. Social media thrives on this kind of casting out. This makes sense as it is easier to see things in others than it is to bear witness to similar traits within ourselves. Internal defense mechanisms offer that protection on a day-to-day basis. After all, how could you continue to function throughout everyday life if you spent your time focusing on all the ways in which you are terrible? Obviously, that is not sustainable or healthy. However, you do need the ability and insight to see yourself more fully. You can only achieve self-acceptance by becoming aware of, and honoring, both the ways in which you are wonderful and the ways in which you can sometimes be difficult and a less likable human being.

This ability to so easily recognize how toxic someone else is may even be a collective toxic trait that we have as humans. Why is it so easy to think of others as mean, difficult, or malicious? Could there be something else, perhaps something deeper, going on within that person just as there is within us?

It should also be said that this dynamic doesn't readily apply to those living with mental illness and chronic self-disparaging thoughts. Mental illnesses like depression (and many other conditions) often come with incredibly inaccurate and debilitating thoughts of self-criticism, which is different from what you're exploring in this exercise. Mental illnesses chronically distort self-perception and often lead those struggling with them to over-identify with self-critical thoughts. It is not uncommon for those living with mental illness to have extremely deflated self-assessments, and hyper-awareness of any less-than-perfect part of themselves. This is not what this exercise is referencing. Of course, it can be hard to discern whether that applies to you or not. If that question is coming up for you now, then it is wise to consult with a licensed therapist for individual support and further clarity.

What traits or behaviors do you most often find yourself annoyed by in others around you? What experiences from your past influences this perception?

What feelings come up for you as you consider these traits and patterns in others? Take a moment to consider how those behaviors or traits apply to you. Do you have a hard time accepting similar patterns within yourself?

What steps can you take to work toward acceptance and self-compassion of your own negative traits? How can you work to extend that same compassion to others in your life around you?

AFFIRMATIONS

It takes courage to become aware of my
own negative traits and patterns.

Doing bad things does not make me a bad person.
Making mistakes is a part of being human.

I can continue to learn about myself and develop
healthier ways of getting my needs met.

SIT WITH DIFFICULT EMOTIONS

One of the most common phrases you might hear come out of the mouths of mental health professionals these days is, "Let's sit with that for a minute." But what does that mean?

"Sitting with" or "making space for" a feeling is the process of giving yourself permission to connect with what you are feeling. This often means taking a moment to identify or label the emotion and sitting in some quiet reflection before moving on to the next talking point or emotion.

Why is this important? First, let's acknowledge how difficult it is to sit with emotions. If you are like most people, then you probably have trouble giving space to the emotions that do not feel overwhelmingly positive. In fact, we collectively relegate any less-than-positive feeling to the recesses of our minds. This means actively avoiding acknowledgment of emotional pain, sadness, hurt, and depression.

Much of this is innate. Your brain works to find ways to reduce or avoid pain. You may notice this come up in your everyday life as you approach a tough feeling and immediately change the subject. You might also over-intellectualize it or minimize the difficult experience entirely ("It wasn't that bad!"). You cut yourself off from connecting to feelings that seem too big to hold and deal with. You avoid the pain altogether. Sitting with that pain means you would have to 1) acknowledge the pain that you've experienced, and 2) accept your own vulnerability—this is hard to do.

You may struggle with viewing vulnerability as weakness. Part of you may think creating space for your feelings means that you are too sensitive or are wallowing in that pain. Under the guise of "moving on" you might overcompensate. You forge ahead with toxic positivity and hyper-resilience. The big problem with that is that the pain hasn't gone anywhere at all. You've just pushed it down and banished it to the shadow.

Ironically, it is often this process that causes the most long-term problems. When you don't create adequate space (and that space is hard to define for each individual person) to process these difficult feelings and experiences, they leak into your day-to-day life. This buried pain might lead you to overcompensate in other areas of your life as you seek protection and restitution in completely inappropriate, and ineffective, ways.

These reflections offer you some of that space to identify emotions that you have a difficult time honoring in your life. Try to envision how you might approach them differently moving forward.

What emotions do you find that you often too quickly bounce back or move on from? What history do you have with these feelings? Whether it's anger, jealousy, sadness, or any other emotion, take a moment now to reflect on previous times when you've felt similar emotions. What happened? Who was involved? Do you feel that you've adequately healed and accepted those experiences? In what ways are you still held captive by them?

How did you process difficult emotions when you were younger? Would you say that your reaction to those feelings has changed at this stage of your life? Why or why not?

What might help you continue to process and accept these difficult emotions or past experiences more fully? Take a few moments to identify at least one strategy or skill that might help you practice sitting with difficult emotions moving forward.

AFFIRMATIONS

I am not flawed for experiencing negative
emotions. Being human means experiencing
a range of feelings and emotions.

It is normal and okay to be impacted
by the things that I experience.

There is no such thing as wallowing,
only the need for more healing.

I can, and will, create more space for
difficult feelings moving forward.

DEAL WITH CONFRONTATION

How willing are you to address confrontation head-on?

Confrontation is not a pleasant experience. For many of us it brings up a lot of negative emotions, especially when it comes to addressing those closest to us.

What is it that makes it difficult for you to express yourself in these situations? Let's start by examining how you felt about seeing the word "confrontation" written here on this page. What immediate thoughts and feelings came up for you? Do you have any impulse to move on to the next section? Were you immediately interested in learning more? The responses to these questions are a good place to start as you reflect here.

You might think of confrontation, or interpersonal conflict, as something to avoid at all costs. It is unpleasant and uncomfortable. At worst, perhaps you fear that standing up for yourself will damage the relationship beyond repair. You may believe that the other person will get out of control in their response to you. You might even think that you'll be the one to fly off the handle in a fit of rage and do something you will immediately regret.

Confrontation is a necessary evil to get closer to some point of resolution. And in that way, confrontation isn't very evil at all, but more so a productive (albeit uncomfortable) step forward. For example, if a loved one says something that hurts you deeply you have two choices: either you can address the problem or swallow your perspective and keep going about your day. One choice creates a path toward potential resolution, while the other all but guarantees those words will continue to impact you for the rest of that day, perhaps even longer. When that happens, where does all the hurt and agitation go? Your shadow. This can lead to growing resentment, passive-aggressiveness, and other ways of acting out. Over time, this kind of behavior degrades relationships and mental health, from within. Momentary peace, while easier, can dismantle the stable foundation of your relationship.

When you think of the word "confrontation" what thoughts or feelings immediately come up for you?

How do those thoughts and feelings impact your ability, or willingness, to confront someone who has wronged you?

Think of the last time that someone confronted you about something that you'd said or done. How did that feel for you? How did you respond?

What do you think you need to better address conflict head-on? What resources might help you progress in this way?

AFFIRMATIONS

Confrontation is often scary and
uncomfortable. It is normal to fear it.

I can feel anxious and hesitant to
assert myself and still do it.

Confrontation is a tool to help better meet
my needs and express boundaries.

Confronting someone who has hurt me is one
way to practice self-care and compassion.

LET JOY COME TO YOU

When most people think of the shadow, they think about all the negative things that they have experienced and buried in their lives. This part of the psyche is all about what is unconscious or not always visible in our lives. However, the shadow isn't just about the dark thoughts and feelings that you experience. It also houses some of the positive parts of you that have become tucked away. For some people, this manifests in the difficulty of experiencing personal joy and happiness.

We, collectively, have a grave misunderstanding about the nature of joy and happiness. You may have felt the pressure to always think and feel positively. This is certainly reinforced by so many of the ideas and conversations that exist out in the world. How often have you shared some difficulty in your life only to find someone responding with some simple platitude like "Just be patient. Everything will work out in the end." In an attempt to be supportive, people can inadvertently teach you that the only acceptable feelings to have are the nice and hopeful ones. These discussions often reinforce the idea that for you to be a likeable and acceptable member of society, you need to present as happy and joyful as much as possible. This is an impossible standard to live up to.

This often creates an unexpected, inverse problem. In your efforts to continuously perform joy and positivity you get farther away from what it means to be joyful. As you work hard to chase this ever-elusive positive state of being, you become preoccupied by it, ironically only furthering yourself from actually feeling it. You learn to seek what others have told you is joy. You fail to define joy for yourself. This means you perpetually fail at being joyful. This breeds guilt and shame. The culture of toxic positivity demands a level of perfection that no one can achieve.

You may often overcorrect to feel joyful. Sometimes this search provides the catalyst for quick dopamine hits in many places like social media, online shopping, and other destructive choices. What you don't often realize, however, is that this search costs you too much. It continues to move the needle from connecting with yourself and the things, people, and experiences that bring you your own special sense of joy. You must also remember that joy is an emotion just like any other. It is transient. Joy is not a continuous state of being.

How do you define joy? What is its place in your life on a day-to-day basis?

What have you learned from the people around you about what it means to be joyful?

Who helps you more fully embrace joy? Are there things (such as objects or activities) that help you reconnect to this part of yourself?

AFFIRMATIONS

Joy is one feeling (among all the other emotions) I have access to.

I do not need to work hard to cultivate joy. I can choose joy by reconnecting with myself and the things that make me feel happy.

I deserve joy and peace in a way that works for me.

APPENDIX A
Jung's Theory of the Psyche

Much of what we understand about personality and the human psyche has its roots in the work of early psychoanalysts like Carl Jung. As he founded analytical psychology and built upon Sigmund Freud's understanding of psychoanalysis, Jung conceptualized the psyche as the entirety of a person's psychic parts—a blend of the mind (thoughts and ideas), spirit, and soul.

With his theory of the psyche, Jung sought to make sense of our internal worlds, which he framed as being made up of both conscious and unconscious parts. He conceptualized the human psyche as the entirety of the Self, which combines not only the conscious and unconscious parts of who wc are but also attempts to address how we navigate those differences in our internal and external worlds.

The role of consciousness—which you may have gathered throughout this book—is both personal and collective. Jung believed that we all have a collective unconscious that is responsible for some of the material that we all share within our psyches. This is most evident in how we come to think of themes that occur within and across cultures and societies. One example is the depiction of the battle between good and evil, which is often represented by lightness and darkness, respectively. Because many of us hold this same paradigm, it's reasonable to assume these meanings are a part of our collective unconscious.

On the other hand, there are ideas that are explicitly a part of collective consciousness. Often these ideas are attached to nationalism and consciously identifying with group membership. For example, if asked, most Americans can offer a similar idea of what it means to be "patriotic" (although that definition shifts somewhat every day). This is a collective conscious identity with its own inherent values and assumptions.

We also have the personal consciousness/unconscious dichotomy within us. Your personal consciousness is how you tend to see yourself, both internally and in relation to others. Consider what roles and adjectives you might use to describe yourself. You might readily identify with a familial or occupational role as a part of your personal consciousness. The adjectives you use to describe yourself to someone else (assertive, kind, tough, resilient, and so on) would also fall under personal consciousness.

Your personal unconscious, by contrast, are those things that you tend to keep hidden about yourself (both from yourself and others). This is shadow material. It's the part of yourself that you attempt to tuck away from others, often to protect others from figuring out just how terrible and flawed you believe yourself to be. This is also the part of you that you have a hard time acknowledging to yourself. You use defenses like denial, repression, and projection (among others) to regulate your feelings about how you see yourself. You also use these defenses to manage how you allow other people to see you (your "persona").

Jung identified the ego as the great moderator of the psyche—the structure responsible for how you identify. It is the proverbial "I." From the time that you're born, you grow in your understanding of what "I" means by interacting with the world around you. Your ego is developed by all your early experiences, thoughts, feelings, and sensations, which give you an understanding of your place in the world. As you continue to grow, so does the ego. The ego helps you craft and learn to use a persona to interact with others in the world around you. The persona is how you show your ego to others. You might think of your persona (and external personality) as the performer side of the ego. Its goal is to demonstrate to the outside world how you see yourself and how you want to be seen. The persona is manifested in the ways that you talk, act, and express yourself (hair, dress, gender, and so on) to the outside world.

By contrast, the shadow (personal unconscious) is the side of you that hides. It's unclear if this need to hide is essential to the shadow itself, or (much more likely) a conscious effort on the part of the ego to disidentify with the undesirable parts. That is, the ego (the "I") likely doesn't want to identify with the shadow parts of the psyche as those irredeemable parts likely threaten the ego's construction of the persona (the face that you show the world).

This makes shadow work very difficult. As you start shadow work, you consciously invite the ego to rest while you give yourself permission to visit with, and hopefully integrate, your shadow parts. But the ego doesn't really want shadow work to happen, so it defends itself from your darker thoughts, feelings, and impulses. It wants to ensure that our persona stays intact, as that likely means survival of itself (the ego). It is hard for you to begin to see all the darker, hidden parts—the ways you don't like to see yourself. But shadow work is as liberating as it is difficult.

Therefore, shadow work is often life-changing since it makes you change the way you see yourself. And once faced with all your darkness, you are forced to carve out a new self-image...a new ego. Do you simply become all those dark impulses? Has the persona been a complete lie and fabrication? What do you do now?

This is both the gift and the curse of shadow work. By working through and accepting the darker parts of yourself, you can experience a new level of inner peace and self-compassion. However, the path there is often fraught with very difficult thoughts and feelings, which is why it is so critical to have tools for grounding, and other social supports, to bolster you.

In Jung's theory of the psyche, the goal of shadow work is to achieve psychological wellness and mental health, most often through the means of analysis and integration. He believed that if you could gain insight into consciousness (personal and collective, conscious and unconscious), you could work to integrate all your internal dynamics and live in peace as a functioning member of society. This is why we do shadow work. It brings hope for a sense of peace and a life of ease. It's an attempt to practice deep self-love, which empowers you to love all the others in your life with the same sense of acceptance.

Further Explanation of Attachment Styles

A Major Factor Regarding Attachment Style

It is hard to quantify how much of someone's attachment style is due to inherent characteristics (nature) or to learned behaviors and feelings (nurture). However, we know that the quality of parenting is a major factor in how children develop attachment to, and feel safe around, others. Parents who more consistently meet the physical and psychological needs of children are more likely to help children develop more secure attachment styles. Inconsistent attunement to the child's needs increases the risk of developing any other attachment style (ambivalent-insecure, avoidant-insecure, or disorganized-insecure).

Additionally, further research shows that children who experience extremely inconsistent attunement (and/or parental absence) are more likely to develop disorganized attachment styles and feel unsure of how to successfully navigate and feel stable in adult relationships. The foundation of contemporary knowledge in this area is developmental psychologist Mary Ainsworth's "Strange Situation" research in which very young children (12–18 months) were observed as they engaged with their mother, had the mother leave them, became acquainted with a stranger, and then reunited with the mother. The infants were observed by researchers and behaviors were coded on how the child responded to the mother leaving, the introduction of the stranger, being left alone with the stranger, and reuniting with the mother. Researchers looked at the child's behavior through these different events, like whether or not the child played in the room, explored the space, searched for Mom, avoided or interacted with the stranger, and so forth. Throughout the experiment, researchers also noted any emotional responses that reflect the child's mood (like smiling, crying, laughing, and so on). This all helped form what we have come to know about attachment styles.

Secure Attachment

In Ainsworth's research, infants who were securely attached to their caregivers responded well to the reunion after the brief separation. They more readily re-engaged with the parent and received the necessary support and nurturance to recover from the separation.

In adult relationships, people who are more securely attached tend to be dependable and reliable partners. They expect and readily cope with relationship challenges and inevitable moments of distance, and generally feel comfortable getting close to others.

Ambivalent-Insecure (Anxious) Attachment

In the research, infants with ambivalent-insecure attachment were very wary of the stranger in the scenario and experienced distress when they were left without their primary caregiver. Upon reunion, they were readily soothed by the parent's return.

As adults, people who are insecurely attached experience more anxiety, particularly in intimate relationships. It is common for anxiously attached adults to worry whether their partner loves them. They may also be reluctant to enter close relationships and routinely seek reassurance.

Avoidant-Insecure (Dismissive-Avoidant) Attachment

Infants with the avoidant-insecure attachment style tended to seek out comfort from the parent figure, but didn't respond very favorably to the comfort that was provided. They also demonstrated no preference on connecting with the parent (versus the stranger) upon reunion.

Adults with avoidant (or dismissive) attachment tend to view close relationships and emotions as relatively unimportant. They may actively avoid close relationships and may not be forthcoming about their feelings, instead opting for more (rather than less) emotional distance. They may often be described as "cold" interpersonally.

Disorganized-Insecure (Fearful-Avoidant) Attachment

The disorganized-insecure attachment style was introduced after John Bowlby's and Ainsworth's work by fellow psychologists Mary Main and Judith Solomon. In their findings, children with disorganized attachment tended to respond in a mixture of avoidant and anxious ways. This often meant the child experienced confusion about their role in the child-parent dynamic, later taking on the role of caregiver. This style is often observed in children who experienced early childhood trauma, neglect, or abuse (and inconsistent parental nurturance).

Adults who have a more disorganized attachment style may often feel confused about how to navigate intimacy even when their own desires are for closeness. Relationships often feel unstable, like an emotional roller coaster. Unlike the strictly avoidant types, disorganized types want close relationships but aren't quite sure how to maintain them.

Further Resources and Readings

For Those Looking for More Support

There is great emotional and psychological risk when doing shadow work. Whenever you take on personal development, particularly shadow work, you come face-to-face with emotions and thoughts that are challenging and require some further attention. While this book is designed to help you begin (or continue) this kind of self-exploration, it can be difficult to do this work alone. As such, as you have made your way through these exercises, you may have considered that you would benefit from some ongoing support. My goal here is to offer you some starting points to look for that support, as well as offer some other books and resources that could help as you continue your journey forward.

If you are looking for professional support, the presence of a licensed therapist is incredibly valuable. I think that self-help is extremely useful in doing shadow work, but sometimes having your own personal guide can make all the difference. A therapist can be a great resource to provide you with customized and individualized support meant to guide you no matter where you are in this specific moment and time in your healing.

There are a few ways to go about finding a professional to work with: word-of-mouth recommendations, sourcing providers through personal research, or receiving a referral from another healthcare provider or insurer. Word-of-mouth referrals are typically best, so if you have a friend or loved one that is working with a therapist or other professional guide, I encourage you to speak with them about their experiences and if they think you two might be a good fit. Alternatively, other licensed health providers typically know of local therapists in their area who might be able to support your efforts and may be able to put you in touch with someone they think may be able to help.

If you search on your own for a provider, the Internet can be an incredibly helpful (but also overwhelming) place. Try searching for any specific issue that you're looking for support on and your zip code. For instance, a search term could read like "licensed therapist trauma 92107" or "local therapist shadow work." Here are some helpful psychology directory sites, including those for folks who often have a hard time finding competent or affirming providers.

Psychology Today
www.psychologytoday.com/us

Directory website that enables you to search by location and provider type (therapist, psychiatrist, psychologist, and so on). You are also able to filter by cost, insurance provider, presenting concern, and a host of other options.

American Psychoanalytic Association
https://apsa.org/find-an-analyst

Search tool to help potential clients seek out psychoanalysts within their local area.

Therapy for Black Girls
https://therapyforblackgirls.com/

Popular directory site and resource that prioritizes helping Black women secure support from licensed mental health providers.

Latinx Therapy
https://latinxtherapy.com/

California-based (but nationwide) directory site and hub for those hoping to connect with providers who self-identify as Latinx/Latino/Latina and support the mental health of members of those communities.

National Queer & Trans Therapists of Color Network
https://nqttcn.com/en/

Nationwide directory of licensed therapists who self-identify as queer and trans people of color (QTPoC).

Additional Reading
It should be noted that therapy isn't always accessible to everyone for a variety of reasons, nor is it the only path toward healing and integration. Many people use several paths to

personal development (I personally have myself), and if you are looking for additional self-help options, there are plenty of books or other resources that could be helpful to you. With that in mind, please remember that not every strategy, book, or professional works for every person.

Sometimes you need to exercise more patience in finding the right outlets for your needs, and that's okay. If something listed in this section doesn't work for you, that's perfectly fine! It may not work for you at this current stage in your life, or it may not fit with you at all. Give yourself permission to pivot and try out new options that you think may work for you. There are no right or wrong answers, only resources that work best for you and others that don't.

Here are some books that I think could be helpful:

The Body Remembers: The Psychophysiology of Trauma and Trauma Treatment by **Babette Rothschild**

Helpful resource by social worker Babette Rothschild that provides both counselors and clients with information regarding the biological and physiological nature of trauma and trauma healing.

Meeting the Shadow: The Hidden Power of the Dark Side of Human Nature by **Connie Zweig and Jeremiah Abrams (editors)**

A collection of written works from mental health professionals (including Jung), researchers, and thought leaders on the concept of the shadow and its impact on our lives.

The Archetypes and the Collective Unconscious: Collected Works of C.G. Jung, Vol.9, Part 1 by C.G. Jung, translated by R.F.C. Hull

A landmark text that captures much of Jung's most popular work and theories. It includes discussions on the shadow, psyche, and collective unconscious.

What We May Be: Techniques for Psychological and Spiritual Growth Through Psychosynthesis by Piero Ferrucci

A comprehensive resource that offers education on psychological and spiritual concepts based on the theory of psychosynthesis to resolve intrapersonal conflicts.

Compassion Cards: Teachings for Awakening the Heart in Everyday Life by Pema Chödrön

Card deck with fifty-nine compassion cards to help you reconnect with personal and collective compassion and commentary by guide Pema Chödrön.

Daring Greatly: How the Courage to Be Vulnerable Transforms the Way We Live, Love, Parent, and Lead by Brené Brown

In this popular book, Brené Brown deftly discusses her research on shame and vulnerability, two themes that appear frequently in shadow work.

Bibliography

Ainsworth, Mary D., et. al. *Patterns of Attachment: A Psychological Study of the Strange Situation.* New York: Psychology Press, 2015.

Corsini, Raymond J., and Danny Wedding. *Current Psychotherapies, Eighth Edition.* Belmont, CA: Brooks/Cole, 2008.

Peluso, Paul R., Jennifer P. Peluso, JoAnna F. White, and Roy M. Kern. "A Comparison of Attachment Theory and Individual Psychology: A Review of the Literature." *Journal of Counseling & Development* 82, no. 2 (Spring 2004): 139–145. https://dx.doi.org/10.1002/j.1556-6678.2004.tb00295.x.

PsychAlive. "What Is Your Attachment Style?" *PsychAlive.* Accessed January 7, 2022. www.psychalive.org/what-is-your-attachment-style/.

Zweig, Connie, and Jeremiah Abrams (editors). *Meeting the Shadow: The Hidden Power of the Dark Side of Human Nature.* New York: Tarcher/Penguin, 1991.

Index